TRADITIONS OF CHRISTIAN SPIRITUALITY

SILENCE AND WITNESS

TRADITIONS OF CHRISTIAN SPIRITUALITY SERIES

SILENCE AND WITNESS

The Quaker Tradition

MICHAEL L. BIRKEL

SERIES EDITOR:
Philip Sheldrake

ORBIS BOOKS
Maryknoll, New York 10545

Founded in 1970, Orbis Books endeavors to publish works that enlighten the mind, nourish the spirit, and challenge the conscience. The publishing arm of the Maryknoll Fathers & Brothers, Orbis seeks to explore the global dimensions of the Christian faith and mission, to invite dialogue with diverse cultures and religious traditions, and to serve the cause of reconciliation and peace. The books published reflect the views of their authors and do not represent the official position of the Society. To learn more about Maryknoll and Orbis Books, please visit our website at www.maryknoll.org.

First published in Great Britian in 2004 by
Darton, Longman and Todd Ltd
1 Spencer Court
140-142 Wandsworth High Street
London SW18 4JJ

First published in the USA in 2004 by
Orbis Books
P.O. Box 308
Maryknoll, New York 10545-0308
U.S.A.

Orbis ISBN 1–57075–518–3

Scripture quotations in this publication are taken from the New Revised Standard Version © 1989, 1995. Division of Christian Education of the National Council of the Churches of Christ in the United States of America.

Printed and bound in Great Britain.

Library of Congress Cataloguing-in-Publication Data

Birkel, Michael Lawrence.
   Silence and witness: the Quaker tradition / Michael L. Birkel.
      p. cm. – (Traditions of Christian spirituality series)
Includes bibliographical references.
   ISBN 1–57075–518–3
   1. Spiritual life—Society of Friends.   2. Spirituality—Society of Friends.
   3. Society of Friends—Doctrines.   I. Title.   II. Traditions of Christian
   spirituality.
      BX7738.B57   2004
      289.6—dc22

                                                         2003021604

To my children,
Anna Margaret and Jonathan.

CONTENTS

PREFACE TO THE SERIES

Nowadays, in the Western world, there is a widespread hunger for spirituality in all its forms. This is not confined to traditional religious people, let alone to regular churchgoers. The desire for resources to sustain the spiritual quest has led many people to seek wisdom in unfamiliar places. Some have turned to cultures other than their own. The fascination with Native American or Aboriginal Australian spiritualities is a case in point. Other people have been attracted by the religions of India and Tibet or the Jewish Kabbalah and Sufi mysticism. One problem is that, in comparison to other religions, Christianity is not always associated in people's minds with 'spirituality'. The exceptions are a few figures from the past who have achieved almost cult status such as Hildegard of Bingen or Meister Eckhart. This is a great pity, for Christianity East and West over two thousand years has given birth to an immense range of spiritual wisdom. Many traditions continue to be active today. Others that were forgotten are being rediscovered and reinterpreted.

It is a long time since an extended series of introductions to Christian spiritual traditions has been available in English. Given the present climate, it is an opportune moment for a new series which will help more people to be aware of the great spiritual riches available within the Christian traditions.

The overall purpose of the series is to make selected spiritual traditions available to a contemporary readership. The books seek to provide accurate and balanced historical and thematic treatments of their subjects. The authors are also conscious of the need to make connections with contemporary experience and values without being artificial or reducing a tradition to one dimension. The authors are well versed in reliable scholarship about the traditions they describe. However, their intention is that the books should be fresh in style and accessible to the general reader.

One problem that such a series inevitably faces is the word 'spirituality'. For example, it is increasingly used beyond religious circles and does not necessarily imply a faith tradition. Again, it could mean substantially different things for a Christian and a Buddhist. Within Christianity itself, the word in its modern sense is relatively recent. The reality that it stands for differs subtly in the different contexts of time and place. Historically, 'spirituality' covers a breadth of human experience and a wide range of values and practices.

No single definition of 'spirituality' has been imposed on the authors in this series. Yet, despite the breadth of the series there is a sense of a common core in the writers themselves and in the traditions they describe. All Christian spiritual traditions have their source in three things. First, while drawing on ordinary experience and even religious insights from elsewhere, Christian spiritualities are rooted in the Scriptures and particularly in the Gospels. Second, spiritual traditions are not derived from abstract theory but from attempts to live out gospel values in a positive yet critical way within specific historical and cultural contexts. Third, the experiences and insights of individuals and groups are not isolated but are related to the wider Christian tradition of beliefs, practices and community life. From a Christian perspective, spirituality is not just concerned with prayer or even with narrowly religious activities. It concerns the whole of human life, viewed in terms of a conscious relationship with God, in Jesus Christ, through the indwelling of the Holy Spirit and within a community of believers.

The series as a whole includes traditions that probably would not have appeared twenty years ago. The authors themselves have been encouraged to challenge, where appropriate, inaccurate assumptions about their particular tradition. While conscious of their own biases, authors have none the less sought to correct the imbalances of the past. Previous understandings of what is mainstream or 'orthodox' sometimes need to be questioned. People or practices that became marginal demand to be re-examined. Studies of spirituality in the past frequently underestimated or ignored the role of women. Sometimes the treatments of spiritual traditions were culturally one-sided because they were written from an uncritical Western European or North Atlantic perspective.

However, any series is necessarily selective. It cannot hope to do full justice to the extraordinary variety of Christian spiritual traditions. The principles of selection are inevitably open to question. I hope that an appropriate balance has been maintained between a sense of the likely readership on the one hand and the dangers of narrowness on the other. In the end, choices had to be made and the result is inevitably weighted in favour of traditions that have achieved 'classic' status or which seem to capture the contemporary imagination. Within these limits, I trust that the series will offer a reasonably balanced account of what the Christian spiritual tradition has to offer.

As editor of the series I would like to thank all the authors who agreed to contribute and for the stimulating conversations and correspondence that sometimes resulted. I am especially grateful for the high quality of their work which made my task so much easier. Editing such a series is a complex undertaking I have worked closely throughout with the editorial team of Darton, Longman and Todd and Robert Ellsberg of Orbis Books. I am immensely grateful to them for their friendly support and judicious advice. Without them this series would never have come together.

PHILIP SHELDRAKE
Sarum College, Salisbury

ACKNOWLEDGEMENTS

This book grows out of many years of teaching and learning, as well as participation in the Religious Society of Friends. I am thankful to colleagues and students at Earlham College and to members of my home meeting, Clear Creek Monthly Meeting. I am especially grateful to the people who read all or some of this work as it evolved: Gwen Halsted, Mary Garman, Stephen Angell, and Stephanie Ford.

Further thanks are due to the following copyright holders for permission to quote:

Pendle Hill Publications, for permission to quote from Mary Garman, Judith Applegate, Margaret Benefiel, and Dortha Meredith (eds.), *Hidden in Plain Sight: Quaker Women's Writings 1650–1700*.

The Library Committee of Britain Yearly Meeting of the Religious Society of Friends, for permission to quote from *The Journal of George Fox*, edited by John L. Nickalls.

Britain Yearly Meeting of the Religious Society of Friends, to quote from *Quaker Faith & Practice: The Book of Christian Discipline of the Yearly Meeting of the Religious Society of Friends (Quakers) in Britain*.

Friends World Committee for Consultation, for permission to quote from *Sharing Our Quaker Faith*, edited by Edwin B. Bronner.

Elise Boulding, for permission to quote from Kenneth E. Boulding, *There Is a Spirit: The Nayler Sonnets*.

Friends United Press for permission to quote from *The Journal and Major Essays of John Woolman*, edited by Phillips P. Moulton.

INTRODUCTION

Therefore, my dear hearts, be faithful every one in your particular measure of God's gift which he hath given you, and on the invisible wait in silence, and patience, and in obedience to that which opens to the mystery of God, and leads to the invisible God, which no mortal eye can reach unto, or behold.[1]

I was sent of God to stand a witness against all violence, and against the works of darkness; and to turn people from darkness to light; and to bring them from the causes of war and fighting, to the peaceable gospel.[2]

Silence and witness are two pillars of Quaker spirituality. Worship in the Quaker tradition is fundamentally receptive and contemplative. Witness is active, testifying to the power of God to transform the human condition and seeking to engage the world to improve human society. At their best, each is rooted in the other: social action can be an expression of worship, and worship can participate in remaking society. For Friends, the experience of divine leading links the two. Our witness grows out of God's leading as encountered in contemplative worship. Faithfulness to leadings, in turn, enhances the experience of worship.

The Religious Society of Friends, or Quakers, arose in an era of spiritual seeking, and this series hopes to address a new generation of seekers. I have come to realize that learning about other spiritual traditions should be an experience of hospitality. I have felt welcomed as a guest while reading other volumes in this series, and I hope that you will feel the same as I welcome you into an exploration of Quaker spirituality. The roots of the English word 'hospitality' lie in the Latin word *hospes*, which means both 'host' and 'guest'. (In fact, if you go back far enough, the roots of the English words for host and guest are similarly related.) What this suggests is that hospitality is not about who gives and who receives. Instead, it is about a relationship of giving and receiving. It is like the spiritual life itself. We welcome God as our guest, though in the end the one whom we invite to make a home in us is the One who is our true home.

Some people who read this book will be other Friends, and I hope that you will enjoy this journey to the trunks of our common attic. The modest dimensions of this book have required me to be selective, yet I hope that in this introduction to our spiritual tradition you will encounter both what is familiar as well as some new or forgotten voices from our heritage.

The interplay of silence and witness has shaped the plan of this book. After an essay on the historical development of Quaker spiritual ideals, the focus turns to Quaker worship. Because testing a leading as to its origin is central to Quaker experience, a discussion of discernment follows. Both meeting for worship and discernment are collective practices, yet the spiritual life embraces private spiritual practices as well, so these are the subject of the next chapter. Witness, in the form of the Quaker testimonies of peace, equality, simplicity and integrity, serves as the focus of the following chapter. Then follows a selection of Quaker voices across the centuries, offering their witness of the spiritual life. The conclusion reflects on what Quaker spirituality may have to offer contemporary spiritual life.

The early Quaker George Fox once described his mission as to take people to Christ and leave them there, so that they may be taught directly by Christ. It is my hope that this modest volume will take readers to early Friends who can then conduct them to their Inward Teacher.

1. SPIRITUAL IDEALS IN QUAKER HISTORY

Friends have described their spiritual goals and practices in different ways over the course of their history. Three hundred and fifty years may be short compared to the eight centuries of the Franciscan legacy or to the Benedictine heritage of a millennium and a half, but it is a long enough time to see change and development as Friends interacted with their surroundings and among themselves in a variety of ways.

The Religious Society of Friends, or Quakers, came to birth amid the excitement and experimentation that accompanied the English Civil War or Puritan Revolution of the mid-seventeenth century. Friends were only one of many radical religious groups that flourished during Oliver Cromwell's rule. Historians have searched far and wide for ancestry of Quakerism, with no consensus emerging among them. Some historians of Quakerism have focused on early Friends' similarities to other social and religious radicals, including left-wing Puritans. Other historians find roots of Quakerism among Anabaptists or see Friends as heirs to continental mystics. Early Quakers bore affinities with all these groups, though direct historical influence has not been fully documented in all these cases. Even when early Quaker religious experience seems mystical, for example, this does not prove contact with other mystical writings or schools of thought. Early Friends saw themselves in prophetic terms and held that their Spirit-led movement was primitive Christianity revived.

George Fox

George Fox was only one of many early leaders among Friends, but he emerged as the most influential and one of the most charismatic. Through his writings, especially his *Journal* which has remained in print from its first publication, he has left his stamp on Quakerism's self-understanding. Probably the Quaker Abraham, he is certainly the Quaker Benedict[1] in the way he shaped the Society of Friends as an orderly community aspiring to spiritual ideals in a practical manner.

Born in 1624 in the undistinguished village of Fenny Drayton in Leicestershire, he grew up as a morally sensitive youth amid the religious searching and military conflicts of the era of the Civil War. The son of a weaver called 'Righteous Christer', and his wife Mary Lago 'of the stock of the martyrs', George Fox was apprenticed to a shoemaker and wool-dealer. As a young man, he left home and wandered, seeking answers to inner trials and temptation to despair. He looked for religious guidance from clergy both in the state-sponsored Church and in separatist Puritan congregations, but neither could provide the help he needed. Finally he discovered the answer within:

> But as I had forsaken all the priests, so I left the separate preachers also, and those called the most experienced people; for I saw there was none among them that could speak to my condition. And when all my hopes in them were gone, so that I had nothing outwardly to help me, nor could tell what to do, then, Oh then, I heard a voice which said, 'There is one, even Christ Jesus that can speak to thy condition', and when I heard it my heart did leap for joy . . . And this I knew experimentally.[2]

This inward experience was a turning point, but temptations to despair continued. In a second major experience, he learned that his efforts to separate himself from evil-doers were misguided in that the dividing line between good and evil ran through every human heart. Fleeing from sinners did not ensure his own moral purity, nor did it enable him to be in relationship with others.

> [The] natures of those things that were hurtful without were within, in the hearts and minds of wicked men . . . though people had been looking without. And I cried to the Lord, saying, 'Why should I be thus, seeing I was never addicted to commit those evils?' and the Lord answered that it was needful that I should have a sense of all conditions, how else should I speak to all conditions; and in this I saw the infinite love of God. I saw also that there was an ocean of darkness and death, but an infinite ocean of light and love, which flowed over the ocean of darkness. And in that also I saw the infinite love of God; and I had great openings.[3]

As a result of this experience, he no longer ran away from people but instead found himself able to engage with them and minister to them. From this point he began his confident travels to share the message of his discovery of the inward availability of God to all. Christ had 'come to teach his people himself'.

In a third significant experience, he felt himself restored to the sinless state of Eden before the first transgression, an ineffable sense of union with God and with creation, the nature of which was revealed or 'opened' to him. Although he did not claim the state for himself, the condition of Christ's enduring perfection revealed itself to him.

> Now I was come up in spirit through the flaming sword into the paradise of God. All things were new, and all the creation gave another smell unto me than before, beyond what words can utter. I knew nothing but pureness, and innocency, and righteousness, being renewed up into the image of Christ Jesus, so that I say I was come up to the state of Adam which he was in before he fell. The creation was opened to me, and it was showed to me how all things had their names given them according to their nature and

virtue . . . I was immediately taken up in spirit, to see into another or more steadfast state than Adam's innocency, even into a state in Christ Jesus, that should never fall . . . Great things did the Lord lead me into, and wonderful depths were opened unto me beyond what can by words be declared; but as people come into subjection to the spirit of God, and grow up into the image and power of the Almighty, they may receive the Word of wisdom, that opens all things, and come to know the hidden unity in the Eternal Being.[4]

A series of 'openings' or divinely disclosed insights provided the substance of George Fox's preaching as he travelled: mere formal education does not qualify one for ministry, he 'was to bring people off' from the mere externals of established religion which were 'forms without power'. These included creeds, ritual, the state-sponsored Church, and paid clergy. Even the Scriptures, though 'very precious'[5] to him, were no longer a final authority: to be understood, they must be read in the Spirit that gave them forth. His task was to bring others to 'Christ their Inward Teacher' who was the 'Light who showed them their sin and brought them through it'. The roots of the Quaker testimonies of equality, integrity, simplicity, and peace lie in these early openings.

In his travels to share this message with other seekers, he met with some success in Yorkshire. Continuing to the northwest he came to Pendle Hill. He felt an inward leading to climb it and to 'sound forth the day of the Lord', echoing Isaiah 40:9. There he had a vision of a great people to be gathered. Finding a receptive audience in nearby settlements, he preached to more than a thousand separatists on Firbank Fell. A regional religious awakening ensued. At the manor of Swarthmoor Hall, he convinced Margaret Fell of the truth of his message, and her home became the centre of the emerging Quaker movement. Her husband, Thomas Fell, a judge, never joined Friends but supported them and protected them in legal matters when he could, until his death in 1658. Swarthmoor Hall became the hub of the early Quaker travelling preachers. They kept regular correspondence with Margaret Fell, and their many letters tell the history of early Friends, both their evangelistic success and the trials of persecution and frequent imprisonment. Margaret Fell's hospitality and administrative gifts nurtured and united the early travelling Friends and played a major role in enabling Quakerism to survive the bitter persecutions of the seventeenth century. Often called the Mother of Quakerism, Margaret Fell earned the epithet.

Her own account of her convincement attests to the inwardness of Quaker spirituality. In Puritan congregations it was common practice to allow someone other than the appointed minister to speak in worship services, often after the cleric offered the sermon. As he did elsewhere, George Fox used this opportunity to offer his insights into the spiritual life to those present at the 'steeple-house' – which is the term early Quakers used to refer to a church building, since they regarded the church as the body of the faithful rather than a physical structure.

> [George Fox] went to Ulverston steeple-house, . . . and when they had done singing, he stood up upon a seat or form, and desired that he might have liberty to speak, and he that was in the pulpit said he might . . . And so he went on, and said, how that Christ was the Light of the world, and lighteth every man that cometh into the world; and that by this light they might be gathered to God, etc. And I stood up in my pew and wondered at his doctrine; for I had never heard such before. And then he went on, and opened the Scriptures, and said, 'The Scriptures were the prophets' words, and Christ's and the apostles' words, and what, as they spoke, they enjoyed and possessed, and had if from the Lord': and said, 'Then what had any to do with the Scriptures, but as they came to the Spirit that gave them forth? You will say, Christ saith this, and the apostles say this, but what canst thou say? Art thou a child of Light, and hast thou walked in the Light, and what thou

speakest, is it inwardly from God?' etc. This opened me so, that it cut me to the heart; and then I saw clearly we were all wrong. So I sat down in my pew again, and cried bitterly; and I cried in my spirit, to the Lord, 'We are all thieves, we are all thieves; we have taken the Scriptures in words, and know nothing of them in ourselves.'[6]

Margaret Fell and George Fox were eventually to marry, eleven years after the death of Thomas Fell. By then the persecution of dissenters raged fiercely, and they, like many Quakers at the time, spent a considerable portion of their married life in separate prisons.

Encountering the Light: The Lamb's War

Over their history, Friends have described the dynamics of the spiritual life in a variety of ways. Consistent, however, has been a pattern of interior struggle, resolution, then reaching outward to change the world.

Early Friends' experience of the Inward Light was not as a cosy fire but rather a relentless search beam that showed them their sinfulness. The Light at first exposed their capacity for evil but then led to the victory of good over evil within them. A sense of inward peace followed – often after a lengthy internal conflict – and a deep sense of community with other Friends who had been through the same harrowing experience. This sense of victory energized them to labour to transform the social order into a godly society. Drawing on imagery from the book of Revelation where Christ is the meek but conquering Lamb, some Friends described this process as 'the Lamb's War'.

Margaret Fell captured the starkness of this experience in a letter in which she urged new Friends to allow the Light to reveal 'the secret subtlety of the enemy of your souls':

> Let the Eternal Light search you, and try you for the good of your souls ... It will rip you up and lie you open, and make all manifest which lodgeth in you ... Therefore all

to this come and by this be searched and judged and led and guided.[7]

The inner struggles of individuals under the searing power of the Light broke forth in physical shaking among some in the earliest days, which is one source of the name 'Quaker', used at first by outsiders in derision of Friends. George Fox offered an alternative explanation, noting that it 'was Justice Bennet of Derby that first called us Quakers because we bid them tremble at the word of the Lord, and this was in the year 1650.'[8]

Quaker historian Hugh Barbour has compared the experience of the Light among early Quakers to the rigours of modern psychotherapy. Friends endeavoured to search out all identifiable levels of self-deception. They realized, for example, that we can escape serious self-scrutiny in an easy, inauthentic self-surrender that then refuses to examine the deeper recesses of self-righteousness. We can try to distance ourselves from sin with a hasty confession that does not thoroughly search out our hidden pride. In our capacity for deceiving ourselves, we can harbour a desperate love of self, then mistakenly imagine that it is the love of God, and make peace with only an imaginary god. The experience of the Light could be terrifying, but a belief that God was ultimately loving gave Friends the strength to endure this inner harrowing.[9]

Influenced by the Gospel of John, early Friends believed that they experienced both judgement and eternal life as beginning in this world.[10] Since they were already living the eschatological life, they dedicated themselves to a more heavenly realm for others as well, a life of integrity, honesty, peace, and simplicity.

While some Friends used the combative imagery of the Lamb's War, others preferred the language of love. Sarah Blackborrow, in the midst of an otherwise rather polemical tract, invited her readers into the experience of God's love. Herself 'having known the terrors of the Lord, and the indignation of the Almighty against all ungodliness', then 'being made a partaker of his everlasting love', she wrote out of that love. Bordering on the ecstatic, her words draw on imagery from Wisdom's house from the book of Proverbs, the mother's house from the Song of Songs, and eschatological metaphors from other biblical sources to capture the power of the intensity and intimacy of the inward life.

> A Love there is which doth not cease, to the seed of God in you all; and therefore doth invite you every one ... to return into it, that into Wisdom's house you may come, where there is a feast provided of things well refined, and the living bread of God is known and fed upon, and the fruit of the Vine drunk of, the unity in the Spirit witnessed, the well-beloved of the Father is here, and this is he who is the fairest of ten thousand, there is no spot nor wrinkle in him; long did my soul thirst after him ... Now all you who thirst after your beloved, come into Wisdom's house ... Oh! love truth and its Testimony, whether its Witness be to you, or against you, love it, that into my Mother's house you all may come, and into the Chamber of her that conceived me, where you may embrace, and be embraced of my dearly beloved one, Love is his Name, Love is his Nature, Love is his life, surely he is the dearest and the fairest.[11]

Not all early Friends kept their ecstasies under control. A tragedy befell early Quakerism in 1656, when prominent preacher James Nayler, apparently urged on by unrestrained followers, rode into the city of Bristol in a symbolic re-enactment of Jesus' entry into Jerusalem. He later claimed that the purpose of the incident was to testify to the Christ within, but the action scandalized many. Charged with blasphemy, he was tried by Parliament and narrowly escaped a death sentence. His punishment can only be described as brutal: he was publicly whipped through London twice with over three hundred strokes each time, his tongue bored through with a hot iron, and his forehead branded with a 'B' for blasphemer. His actions brought all of Quakerism into disgrace and estranged him from other Friends, particularly George Fox. James Nayler endured his dishonour and punishment with quiet courage, came to a deeper degree of humility, and was ultimately reconciled with Friends, including George Fox. His final writings reflected movingly on the experience of God's forgiveness. But the Bristol incident tarnished Quakers in the eyes of others for many years. It prompted Friends to reflect painfully on how to discern genuine leadings.

Persecution, Organization, and Emigration

Early Friends were no strangers to imprisonment during the reign of Oliver Cromwell. George Fox's confident proclamation of the Light Within, for example, offended many. When asked if he were Christ, he responded, 'Nay; we are nothing; Christ is all.'[12] Yet this sounded too close an identification with Christ to authorities, who sentenced him to prison for blasphemy. Other early Quaker leaders spent time in jails, but widespread imprisonment of Quakers began only after the return of the crown.

The Puritan revolution died with Oliver Cromwell, and toleration of religious radicals with it. The English monarchy was restored in 1660, and a vengeful Parliament enacted laws intended to stamp out nonconformity to the established Church. Until the Act of Toleration in 1689, Friends and other dissenters suffered waves of persecution. It was, for example, punishable by law for more than five people to gather and pray unless they used the Anglican *Book of Common Prayer*. Officers of the law would come and arrest whole congregations at worship. In the town of Reading, the children kept the meeting going while all the adults were in jail. Ruinous fines were imposed, of which a third of the money taken would go to the informant, encouraging Quaker-hunting among the unscrupulous.

Suffering came to play a key role in Quaker spirituality, as well as a sense of deeper separation from 'the world's people' who persecuted them. Persecution of Friends during this time was not as severe as that faced by Anabaptists in Europe during the previous century, and so Friends did not develop quite the emphasis on separation from the wider society that characterized some Anabaptist groups such as Mennonites or Hutterites. Thanks in large part to William Penn's colony, Quakers did not cloister themselves completely from the wider world and all of political life. They did, however, withdraw into a more sectarian frame of mind. There came to be a 'hedge' around the Society of Friends, to guard them from a surrounding culture that did not share their values.

A second response to the persecutions was the rise of organization. The rapid growth of Quakerism in its first decade lent a confidence that all of England, and perhaps the wider world, would become Quaker. More precisely, they hoped that all Christians would reform themselves in a Quaker pattern – since the first Quakers did not intend to start a new denomination but to restore primitive Christianity as they saw it. In the succeeding decades Friends realized that clearly the whole world was not going to join them. To survive at all, Friends needed more organization, to make the reluctant shift from a movement to an institution. George Fox and Margaret Fell were the architects of a structured Quakerism. Although formal membership in the Society of Friends arose only in the eighteenth century, the establishment of monthly meetings to conduct business and make decisions set the pattern for group discernment and the disciplined life that characterized Friends in later periods of their history.

A third response to persecution was emigration. Quakers came to the English colonies. Significant Quaker populations emerged in Rhode Island, North Carolina, western New Jersey, and, of course, Pennsylvania, which was home to William Penn's Holy Experiment in religious toleration and peaceful relations.

A Settled Existence

The charismatic intensity of the first generation of Friends gave way to a more subdued Quaker culture of the eighteenth century. The metaphor of the Lamb's War declined in use, but the threefold scheme of interior struggle, resolution, and social change continued.

On the whole, the robust confidence of the earliest Quakers gave way to greater circumspection and to an unrelieved doubt concerning their own purity of motive. The terror of the Lamb's War may have abated, but in its place came an uncertainty that was life-long. This lack of assurance coloured their understanding of the inward life. For earlier Friends, it was essential to attend to the Light throughout life, yet there was a sense that, although they could always choose to fall from grace, the time of judgement had already come and gone. For eighteenth-century Quakers, the cycle of purification and rebirth was repeating. One could go through many interior baptisms.

The letters of Irish Friend Richard Shackleton (1726–92) reflect this strain of Quaker piety:

> The Lord . . . has appeared in my heart at this time, both in public and private, as a refiner with fire, and as a fuller with soap, to the cleansing and purifying of my heart, and fitting it for a temple meet for him to dwell in.[13]

> I have . . . been favoured at times, . . . with the washing of water to repentance and regeneration . . . through the powerful operation of the Spirit of judgment and of burning . . . For as the sheep is washed and cleansed, in order that it may be shorn; so are we washed and cleansed, that we may 'bring forth fruit meet for Him who has dressed.'[14]

> As was said to the mother of our Lord, the begotten of the Father, 'Yea a sword shall pierce through thy own soul also, that the thoughts of many hearts may be revealed.' So it is requisite for those, whose souls are impregnated and made prolific by the Divine Spirit, repeatedly to witness to that Sword, that Word, that fiery law to do its office, so that the vessel may be made clean, and kept clean, fit to contain and to transmit in unadulterated purity the precious odours, and sweet incense, which it may be honoured to convey.[15]

Richard Shackleton's language may strike contemporary ears as harsh and pessimistic. Friends of that era, however, could be optimistic about the soul that experienced purification and regeneration. In his reflections on the central transformation of the spiritual life, colonial New Jersey Quaker John Woolman (1720–72) regarded selfishness and greed as the basic human problem. His view was that, when we are dominated by selfishness and greed, ultimately we are choosing death rather than life. We are estranged from God. But divine love can purify us from this polluted condition that breeds injustice. When we let go of that selfish disposition, allowing it to die, we die and rise with Christ. We then see the nature of God anew. God's love fills our hearts and flows from us to all people. We dedicate our lives to promoting the justice and goodness that God desires for all.[16] In a passage from his *Journal* brimming with biblical allusions, he describes this experience:

'No man can see God and live.' This was spoken by the Almighty to Moses the prophet and opened by our blessed Redeemer. As death comes on our own wills and a new life is formed in us, the heart is purified and prepared to understand clearly. 'Blessed are the pure in heart, for they shall see God.' In purity of heart the mind is divinely opened to behold the nature of universal righteousness, or the righteousness of the kingdom of God. 'No man hath seen the Father save he that is of God; he hath seen the Father.'

The natural mind is active about the things of this life, and in this natural activity business is proposed and a will in us to go forward in it. And as long as this natural will remains unsubjected, so long there remains an obstruction against the clearness of divine light operating in us; but when we love God with all our heart and with all our strength, then in this love we love our neighbours as ourselves, and a tenderness of heart is felt toward all people, even such who as to outward circumstances may be to us as the Jews were to the Samaritans . . . In this love we can say that Jesus is the Lord, and the reformation in our souls, manifested in a full reformation of our lives, wherein all things are new and all things are of God – in this the desire of gain is subjected. And employment is honestly followed in the light of Truth, and people become diligent in business, 'fervent in spirit serving the Lord' – here the name is opened. 'This is the name by which he shall be called: the Lord our Righteousness.'[17]

Divisions

Early Quakers were not Christian by default: there were non-Christian options in seventeenth-century England, such as Ranterism. The theology of early Friends held together in a creative tension both particular and universal elements. It was Christ Jesus who spoke to the condition of George Fox in his time of temptations to despair. Yet Christ was also the Light that enlightens everyone, as Friends read in the first chapter of John's Gospel. So this Inner Light was available to all people, even those who never heard the gospel. The historical event of the cross rendered salvation possible for all human-kind, but in Quaker theology this reality had to be inwardly experienced to be effective for the individual.

This tightly woven fabric that held together the universality of the Light of Christ with the particularity of the life and work of Jesus began to unravel in the nineteenth century. Wider theological currents in the nineteenth century left many Christian bodies divided, and Friends in North America were no exception, though Irish and British Friends escaped a major, enduring schism. The quietist strain in eighteenth-century Quakerism, which had become so suspicious of human initiative, felt spiritually stifling to a new generation. The sectarian impulse felt like an obstacle to co-operation with other Christians on the pressing social challenges of the day, such as anti-slavery work. These elements of Quaker spirituality, regarded as inadequate to the needs of the time, drove some

Friends into conversation with the religious movements that were at the centre of much philanthropic activity in the nineteenth century.

The rival religious trends in Protestant Christianity were rational religion and the evangelical movement. The former appealed chiefly to reason, while the latter gave a significant role to feeling. Integrating head and heart is challenging enough for a single person; doing so as a Church might be much more difficult, at least to judge from the historical record.

Rational religionists were suspicious of feelings. People could allow themselves to get carried away with their emotions, and then havoc could reign. For the rationalists, God was eminently reasonable. God's creation reflected divine rationality. Some rationalists identified the ethical aspects of biblical law with the law of nature; others equated practical morality with worship. The effect of rational religion was to lessen the need for divine revelation: Scripture contained no new information but rather only reminded a forgetful humankind of what was as old as creation itself. One logical result of rational religion was deism, which held that God fashioned the world like a clock maker, setting it in motion and then letting it run on its own.

The universalism of rational religion bore some resemblance to the universalist strain in Quakerism, in the eyes of some.[18] Yet Quakerism held too strongly to the idea that God would lead the faithful into new truth for it to be fully comfortable with important elements of rational religion. Friends believed that revelation was continuing beyond the biblical era, not that biblical revelation itself was redundant. The belief in the availability of God within each person did not fit well with a definition of the divine that left God on some kind of permanent vacation. But there were some places where rational religion did overlap with Quaker concerns for some Friends.

One was the commitment of, for example, many Unitarians to social progress and human justice. Some Quakers worked with Unitarian abolitionists in anti-slavery societies.

A second point of contact was in regard to biblical interpretation. What was a pacifist group to make of the apparently divinely ordained warfare in the Bible? Earlier Christians, from the time of Origen in the third century, preferred to allegorize such accounts, regarding them as symbols of the interior struggle between good and evil, much as early Quakers themselves did in their use of the expression 'the Lamb's War'. Rational religionists, however, held that such biblical passages were simply in error. The Bible was not infallible. Some Friends such as Abraham Shackleton (1752–1818) of Ireland and Hannah Barnard (1754–1825) of New York found such an explanation attractive. For them the loving God revealed in Jesus Christ would never have commanded such violence. Their position collided with the tidal wave of evangelical influence in some Quaker circles.

Protestants in the evangelical movement were also dedicated to philanthropic causes, and many were active in the anti-slavery movement. But their emphasis on the Bible as the centre of religious truth disturbed those Quakers who held, as George Fox had put it, that the Scriptures must be read in the same Spirit that gave them forth. To these Friends, the new evangelical doctrine felt like a return to mere externals. Sarah Lynes Grubb (1773–1842) expressed these concerns:

> Surely the holy scriptures direct us to Christ within, the hope of glory; but *now* we are told, that in looking for *inward* direction, we subject ourselves to error; and that the Gospel is to be found in the scriptures, where there is 'clear, comprehensible truth', and 'a direct message from God.' True, the scriptures come by inspiration of God, yet, in my view, the same inspiration must be with us, to give us to comprehend their spiritual meaning and application; because the natural man, by all his head knowledge and finite capacity, even though he may compare scripture with scripture, and acknowledge to their harmony, is, nevertheless, the natural or unregenerate man still, without the operation of the Spirit in his soul; even that which is the Divine gift to all men, and which, I conceive, brings all who adhere to it, into a converted state, whether they

be favoured with the inspired writings, which tell of the blessed and holy redeemer, or whether they be ignorant of them. Must it not be our experience, in order to partake of the benefit of the death and sufferings of Christ, to be brought into obedience and righteousness? And what can do this for us, but the power of God, or name of Jesus, which is immediately made known to us by inward revelation thereof?[19]

A leading opponent to the rise of evangelical influence among Quakers was Elias Hicks (1748–1830), a respected minister from rural New York who was in his seventies when the controversy grew sharp. For Elias Hicks and others called quietists, to allow the inward Christ to work in the soul, the self must refrain from all willing and acting. The lively fervour of evangelical devotion looked to him like the emotional indulgence of a self whose task was to still itself into self-forgetfulness. His extremely inward spirituality was lofty but austere.

The quietist tradition resembled in some ways the spirituality of the Rhineland mystics of the late Middle Ages, such as Meister Eckhart. The goal was to lose the self in union with God. The soul was to submit itself to annihilation, becoming nothing. If the language used to describe God in this tradition could sound impersonal, it hardly mattered because the ideal was selflessness – there was hardly a self left to be in relationship with a personal God. The soul was a drop of water absorbed in the ocean of Godhead.

The evangelical tradition bore a resemblance instead to the spirituality of the medieval Cistercians, such as Bernard of Clairvaux. Theirs was a love mysticism, focused on the person of Jesus. The evangelical tradition offered to Quaker spirituality a recovery of the full humanity of Jesus. The risk of the Quaker focus on the inwardness of Christ as the Light is that the human qualities of the historic Jesus can become absorbed in the cosmic dimension of the divinity of Christ. This can diminish the warmth of a personal relationship with God as revealed in Jesus. We saw this warmth in the love language of

Sarah Blackborrow earlier in this chapter, but the spirituality of Elias Hicks does not lend itself to this direction. Joseph John Gurney (1788–1847), the leading evangelical voice among English Friends in the first half of the nineteenth century, wrote invitingly of that warmth and tenderness. Like Bernard, he emphasized the humility of Jesus, which arouses our love. Both writers were fond of the Song of Songs as an allegory of the loving union between Christ and the soul.

> Jesus selects for himself a humble station, and a life of poverty. His birth-place is a stable; his cradle a manger; his early home a Galilean village; his mother a virgin, royally descended indeed, but of a low estate; his reputed father, a mechanic . . . When his followers would make him a king, he finds his refuge in the wilderness; he prefers the form of a servant; he ministers to his brethren; he washes his disciples' feet . . . Having made himself of no reputation, he humbles himself yet further – even 'unto death'; and the depth to which he submits, is a public execution, in the form which was appointed for the vilest malefactors. Such were the depths of humiliation to which he descended; but who shall tell the sufferings which he endured? . . . The greater advances we make towards divine purity, the more acute becomes our sympathy with the sufferings of others; the deeper our distress, because of the sinfulness of the world; and the more painful to our feelings, those insinuations and temptations of the devil, with which we are ourselves assailed . . . Our blessed Lord, although clothed in humanity, was *perfectly pure*. How unspeakably tender and acute, therefore, must have been his sympathy with an afflicted generation.[20]

The suffering of Christ awakens in us a sympathy that extends to others who are suffering. For Joseph John Gurney, this motion outward expressed itself particularly in his work to promote the abolition of slavery.

Among North American Friends, a rather uneasy alliance of quietists and those influenced by rationalism conflicted with evangelicals. When mixed with a struggle for political power within yearly meetings, a schism resulted in 1827-8, first in Philadelphia and then spreading throughout North American Quakerism. Friends felt it as a tremendous tragedy: both sides still shared the belief that God would lead the faithful into unity, and yet the conflicting parties could not find reconciliation. To the larger world, the schism must have seemed insignificant or imperceptible. True, other Protestant denominations in the United States were dividing along the same lines regarding the evangelical movement, but the non-doctrinal distinctives of both Quaker parties were the same. Both parties continued to observe meeting for worship in the same manner. Both allowed women to preach. Both followed the same pattern of plain dress, the Quaker uniform. Both continued opposition to slavery and war.

In hindsight we can see how unfortunate it was that the two sides argued past one another, never quite understanding the opponent's point. For one side, the evangelical emphasis on the authority of Scripture and the blood atonement felt like a diminution of the inward-dwelling Christ. For the evangelical, however, it was the Scriptures that made the humanity of Christ available to them, and the atonement was an act of inestimable love rather than an external, mechanical transaction.

Other divisions followed. By mid-century the major factions were the evangelical Gurneyite Friends who took their name from Joseph John Gurney, the quietist Wilburites whose name derived from John Wilbur (1774–1856), and the Hicksites named after Elias Hicks.

The revivals of the 1860s and beyond effected permanent changes in the form of Quaker worship among evangelical Friends. Borrowing from the patterns used in revivals, meetings for worship employed hymns and a planned sermon. Worship among these Friends now resembled that of their Methodist neighbours. Itinerant revivalist preachers attracted people previously unchurched, who then asked the preachers to stay and initiate them more fully into the Christian life that should follow an emotionally powerful conversion. A system of paid Quaker pastors came into being to meet this need. Gurneyite Friends had entered the mainstream of North American evangelical Protestantism.[21]

Among the Gurneyites other developments followed later in the century. Friends influenced by the evangelical revival spoke in terms of conversion. The depraved, fallen condition of humankind meant that the basic human task was to 'get saved'. For some, shaped by the holiness tradition from Wesleyan theology, there was a second blessing that followed salvation, an instantaneous transformation into perfect sinlessness and freedom from temptation. The move to the outer world was now mostly one of mission, in an effort to reach otherwise lost souls in these final days, but the concept of missions grew to include this-worldly services, such as education, health services, and disaster relief.

Evangelical Friends gathered to formulate a common statement of faith in Richmond, Indiana, in 1887. From this conference emerged the Richmond Declaration, much of it crafted by English Friend Joseph Bevan Braithwaite (1818–1905). Consonant with general, non-Quaker evangelical theology, this statement rejected universalism, made no reference to the Light (arguably rejecting the concept), and dismissed the notion of continuing revelation. In harmony with Quaker tradition, it did not endorse the outward sacraments, though it gave tacit approval to the rising system of paid pastors.[22]

Liberalism

British Friends, from Joseph John Gurney in the 1820s, had provided leadership and inspiration for North American evangelical Quakers. By the time that Joseph Bevan Braithwaite had offered a similar service in the 1880s, however, the theological tide was already turning back home in England. Modern liberal theology was in bloom, and British Friends, especially after a momentous conference in Manchester in 1895, joined sympathies with fellow travellers in North America. The harbinger of this movement, a short book entitled *A Reasonable Faith*, shows this new direction. Although it is less strident than some proclamations of Elias Hicks, its theological kinship is clear.

> Now the spirit of the Gospel, as we understand it, is a spirit of *love* and *power*, and of a *sound mind* ... We understand the Bible to be ... the Record of a *Progressive Revealing* of Spiritual Truth; each part adapted in its day to the gradually maturing intelligence of mankind ... nor does the book itself claim that we are to look to the Bible (invaluable as its Spiritual Revelations are) as the sole religious Light and Teaching of the World; nor that the Most High withholds from any living man some measure of the same Divine Influence which 'inspired' the religious element of the Bible ... [The] popular definition of the Doctrine of the Atonement ... says in effect, '*God is angry, and must be propitiated.*' ... How contrary is all this to the beautiful winning spirit of God's reconciling love in Christ, as recorded in the Gospels![23]

Liberal Friends were first influenced by the rationalism of the wider movement of liberal religion. Modernity brought a scientific outlook, an optimism regarding human nature (in response to the revivalists' stress on human sinfulness), and a social Darwinism that held that human society is progressing and evolving toward the better. Complementing this, without consciously contradicting this, came a mystical approach to the spiritual life.

British Friend Caroline Stephen (1834–1909) was one of the first to identify Quakerism as mystical. Earlier Friends had read Christian mystics such as Bernard of Clairvaux and Johannes Tauler with appreciation, but they had not explicitly claimed that Quakerism was in the stream of Christian mysticism. Liberal mystical Quakers developed their own patterns of speaking of spiritual growth.

Rufus M. Jones (1863–1947) was a proponent of the mystical life and the leading voice in Quakerism for the first half of the twentieth century. He shared the liberal, progressive, optimistic spirit of his age. Both a scholar of mysticism and an experienced mystic, he wrote of the spiritual life with a vividness that was contagious. In his understanding of the mystical life, he distinguished negative from affirmative mystics. The negative way stressed withdrawal from the physical world perceived by sense and studied by reason, seeking God through asceticism, and annihilation of the self, striving for the ephemeral moment of ecstasy. The affirmative mystic, on the other hand, valued the physical realm as infused with divine presence. The experience of union with God heightened rather than destroyed human personality, driving the mystic back into the world for service. Rufus Jones regarded the mystical life as no longer the private reserve of the few but as within the reach of all who could trust their intuition of the nearness of the God who dwelt within them. A person of service himself, Rufus Jones was a founder and long-time chairperson of the American Friends Service Committee, whose relief efforts in Europe after the two major wars of the twentieth century earned the agency the Nobel Peace Prize in 1947, which they received on behalf of all Friends. The generation of Rufus Jones brought about a renaissance in Quakerism in study and practice. He reinterpreted Quaker history, portraying Friends as heirs to the medieval continental mystics. Focusing on Quakers' inner experience, rather than on doctrine, he laboured to heal the nineteenth-century divisions among Friends.

Those labours bore significant fruit by mid-century. Quakers from the various branches of North American Friends had been working together on issues of peace and social justice. After over four decades of preparation, Philadelphia's two yearly meetings formally reunited in 1955. While all Friends did not reconcile their theological differences, avenues for dialogue continued to open. The Earlham School of Religion, founded in the 1960s, serves as a place of theological education and spiritual formation for the different branches of Quakerism across the theological spectrum. On a more local level, Margery Post Abbott has in recent years been gathering together liberal and evangelical Quaker women in the Pacific Northwest to pray, engage in dialogue, and work together in service. More globally, the Friends World Committee for Consultation brings together Friends to discover their common ground.

Although scholars have raised questions about how historically precise Rufus Jones was in tracing a mystical pedigree for Quakers, most liberal Friends since the time of Caroline Stephen have continued to identify Quakerism as mystical in orientation. The heirs of Rufus Jones in this regard included Douglas Steere, Thomas Kelly, and Richenda Scott, each of whom wrote engaging works on Quaker spirituality. A renaissance of Quaker spirituality continues through the work of William Taber, Patricia Loring, Rex Ambler, and others. Because evangelical Friends in the twentieth century carried on a vigorous mission work, numerically most successful in Kenya and Bolivia, it may well be Friends whose first language is not English who shape important new directions for the twenty-first century.

2. MEETING FOR WORSHIP

Meeting for worship is the heart of Quaker spirituality. Everything else in the spiritual life flows into meeting for worship, and all of Quaker spirituality flows out of it.

The Quaker faith is above all experiential. Although some have been initially attracted by Quaker ethics, such as the peace testimony, or specific Quaker beliefs, it is the experience of worship that persuades one that Society of Friends is her or his spiritual home. The early Quaker theologian Robert Barclay attested to the convincing power of this inward – or as he put it, 'secret' – experience when he wrote:

> when I came into the silent assemblies of God's people I felt a secret power among them which touched my heart, and as I gave way unto it, I found the evil weakening in me and the good raised up, and so I became thus knit and united unto them, hungering more and more after the increase of this Power and Life whereby I might feel myself perfectly redeemed.[1]

A more modern voice, that of Caroline Stephen (1834–1909), attests to the attracting power of meeting for worship:

> On one never-to-be-forgotten Sunday morning, I found myself one of a small company of silent worshippers who were content to sit down together without words, that each one might feel after and draw near to the Divine Presence, unhindered at least, if not helped, by any human utterance. Utterance I knew was free, should the words be given; and, before the meeting was over, a sentence or two

were uttered in great simplicity by an old and apparently untaught man, rising in his place amongst the rest of us. I did not pay much attention to the words he spoke, and I have no recollection of their purport. My whole soul was filled with the unutterable peace of the undisturbed opportunity for communion with God, with the sense that at last I had found a place where I might, without the faintest suspicion of insincerity, join with others in simply seeking His presence. To sit down in silence could at the least pledge me to nothing; it might open to me (as it did that morning) the very gate of heaven . . . the place of the most soul-subduing, faith-restoring, strengthening, and peaceful communion, in feeding upon the bread of life, that I have ever known.[2]

Quaker meeting is as simple as it is complex. The community gathers together in a waiting, expectant frame of spirit. Worship is in silence until a participant feels led to share a message with those present. There may be many, few, or no such messages, which Friends call 'vocal ministry'. The meeting concludes when the person with responsibility for closing the worship discerns that the time has drawn to an end. In many parts of the Quaker world, worshippers then shake hands with those around them.

It is as simple as flying a jet: you take off, you go somewhere, you land; you quiet yourself, you encounter God, you refresh and perhaps redirect your life. The complexities are familiar ones to many spiritual traditions: arriving at stillness of body and mind, discernment, and the dimensions of community life in the body of Christ.

Stillness

To sit in silence is often to notice how unsilent the world is and how unstill one's body is. Friends have approached this challenge in many ways. Tayeko Yamanouchi, writing in 1979, recommended her gentle appreciation for the external world.

As I silence myself I become more sensitive to the sounds around me, and I do not block them out. The songs of the birds, the rustle of the wind, children in the playground, the roar of an airplane overhead are all taken into my worship. I regulate my breathing as taught me by my Zen friends, and through this exercise I feel the flow of life within me from my toes right through my whole body. I think of myself like the tree planted by the 'rivers of water' in Psalm 1, sucking up God's gift of life and being restored.[3]

What otherwise would be distractions can be woven into a prayerful frame of mind. A baby's babbling moves one to joy and gratitude for newness of life. A neighbour's coughing inspires a prayer for her health. Gladly received, such sounds lose their potential to distract, so the task is to cultivate a disposition of grateful receptivity.

Once the outer world that comes to us through the senses ceases to disturb, the attention turns inward. The human mind is a perpetual thought mill, so the task of interior stillness poses a significant challenge. Because they have always insisted on the centrality of immediate divine guidance, Friends have been somewhat reluctant to articulate with detail their methods for the spiritual life. Quakers have historically preferred to show rather than to tell. Early Friend Isaac Penington wrote, 'This is the manner of their worship. They are to wait upon the Lord, to meet in the silence of flesh, and to watch for the stirrings of his life, and the breakings forth of his power amongst them,'[4] but his words do not tell us how to do just that. Across the centuries Friends have practised a variety of methods to 'centre down' in the silence of worship.

Some methods focus on the potential distractions themselves. The worshipper may invite the worries, excitements, and desires to present themselves, then gently dismiss each one, acknowledging its role in the worshipper's life and agreeing to return to them after the time of worship. Then, if these thoughts return during meeting for worship, they are recognized in advance before they have completely absorbed the worshipper's attention.

Others may take time to pray for the causes of those thoughts, be it a personal relationship, a crisis, or an international conflict. If the first method is gently to send distractions down the river with a promise to return to them later, the second is to set them in the lap of God, trusting that they will be cared for. Neither method regards distractions as an enemy to be combated forcefully.

As the worshipper enters a state of initial calm, often there comes a natural movement toward prayer. Christian prayer has its apophatic and kataphatic dimensions: some forms of prayer seek to empty the mind of thoughts in order to make room in the heart for God; other forms of prayer employ our capacity to reflect and to imagine as routes to an increased awareness of divine presence. Quakers have used both to centre down. Robert Barclay points worshippers in an apophatic direction: 'Each made it to their work to retire inwardly to the measure of grace in themselves, and not being only silent as to words, but even abstaining from all their own thoughts, imaginations and desires.'[5]

Elias Hicks spoke the following words in 1826. Like Robert Barclay, his goal was to silence both thoughts and desires, both discursive and volitional activities.

> I felt nothing when I came into this meeting, nor had I a desire after anything but to center down into abasement and nothingness; and in this situation I remained for a while, till I found something was stirring and rising in my spirit. And this was what I laboured after; to be empty, to know nothing, to call for nothing, and to desire to do nothing.[6]

Other Friends have found it more congenial to use words and images in their prayer of centring. Some have repeated passages from Scripture, such as lines from a psalm or the Lord's Prayer, dwelling on the feelings of awe, gratitude, and praise that such words evoke. Others may use a phrase like a mantra, as does contemporary centring prayer, as a way of focusing the mind and consenting to God's presence.[7]

Prayers of praise can bring some into a powerful sense of the presence of God. Others may find their way to God through other people and so begin by praying for those in the room, asking that God's mercy, light, and love may feel abundantly present in their lives.

In our word-saturated era, some find that images are a more direct route to enhanced sense of God's presence. Earlier Quakers did not make use of artistic images in devotion, such as paintings or sculpture, yet the images from Scripture nourished their souls. Some Friends have found their way to the centre within through images of the living water, the lamb of God, the rose of Sharon, or the lilies of the field. Images of Christ on the cross or triumphantly risen, pictured inwardly, have aided some on the path to the centre. I know a Friend who centres down with an image of Jesus washing the feet of all in the room. Images can serve as a focus for the mind, so that the inner eye can gaze upon God in simple, loving receptivity. Or the imagination can be more active, as when one imagines oneself taking part in a biblical story, playing a role in the interior drama and encountering God afresh in that moment.

These various methods, in the context of Friends in meeting for worship, are means, not ends. They are transitional; their purpose is to bring worshippers into an increased awareness of God's presence in the worshipping community. Some experienced Friends use none of these tools and simply attend, in a relaxed yet focused way, to their deep inward desire to be present to God.[8]

As worshippers centre, two things occur. First, they find that they are given what to focus their minds on. When successful in avoiding the ever-present pitfall of self-deception, this stage of worship feels genuinely Spirit-led, rather than predetermined by the worshipper. It may be a wordless sense of divine presence, an effortless tranquillity. Others may experience

images of many sorts, possibly scenes from their lives that feel
in need of attention – though the particular events on their
minds feel given by God rather than driven by whatever external worries they may have brought to the meeting for worship.
Some may feel an insight into a matter. Others may find the
events on their minds painful, perhaps a difficult truth to face
about themselves, a troubling interior place that stands in
need of redemption or healing.

The early Friends spoke of the Lamb's War, the inner
struggle between good and evil, the conflict between the righteousness of God and human sinfulness. The same Light of
Christ that led them to peace first revealed to them their
conflicts and contradictions. Early Quakers found their first
experience of this to be a harrowing, life-changing encounter.
Later, such revelations were not as unravelling, as Friends
grew in trust of the Light, and as they felt the loving presence
of God surrounding these otherwise uncomfortable disclosures.

The Collective Dimension of Worship

Second, as worshippers centre, they become aware of the collective dimension of their worship. Worship in community is
more than prayer in solitude. It is not simply common purpose
but a felt sense of togetherness that joins worshippers. We can
experience one another at depths that challenge our ability to
describe them. As put by Beatrice Saxon Snell, 'those who per-
severe in group worship know that it differs from private devotion as the music of an orchestra differs from the music of a
single player.'[9] George Fox urged Friends to 'Mind that which
is eternal, which gathers your hearts together up to the Lord,
and lets you see that you are written in one another's hearts.'[10]
His words echo those of the apostle Paul in 2 Corinthians 3,
where he speaks of being 'written on human hearts' with the
'Spirit of the living God'. In worship, this living God draws us
together in love and gives a knowledge of one another in that
togetherness.

A member of my own meeting once compared centring in

worship to a magnet. First, like a magnet dangling on a string, the soul must be free to find its true north. Then as one sinks more deeply into worship, one can serve as a magnet, powerfully attracting others into the experience of God's presence. Simply by being worshipfully present in a deeply centred place, and yet in relationship with other worshippers, one can draw them toward inward depths.

Robert Barclay employed the image of many candles joined together:

> As many candles lighted and put in one place do greatly augment the light, and makes it more to shine forth; so when many are gathered together into the same Life, there is more of the glory of God, and his power appears to the refreshment of each individual for that he partakes not only of the Light and Life raised in himself but in all the rest.[11]

Writing over 200 years later, Caroline Stephen expressed the same experience, noting how stillness flows 'from vessel to vessel':

> In the united stillness of the truly 'gathered' meeting, there is a power known only by experience, and mysterious even when familiar. There are perhaps few things which more readily flow 'from vessel to vessel' than quietness. The presence of fellow-worshippers in some gently penetrating manner reveals to the spirit something of the nearness of the Divine Presence.[12]

Spoken words have always played a significant role in meeting for worship, but Friends minister to one another in the silence as well. As the worshippers settle, it can happen that some sensitive souls can feel the state of the worship of the community as a whole or of particular worshippers. In prayer they draw the others toward God's healing presence, where their inward conflicts can be resolved. Robert Barclay put it this way:

> Each made it their work to retire inwardly to the measure
> of Grace in themselves . . . They come thereby to enjoy and
> feel the arisings of this Life, which, as it prevails in each
> particular, becomes as a flood of refreshment and over-
> spreads the whole meeting . . . and so there being also an
> inward quietness and retiredness of mind, the witness of
> God ariseth in the heart, and the Light of Christ shineth
> whereby the soul cometh to see its own condition . . . and
> thus we are often greatly strengthened and renewed in the
> spirits of our minds without a word, and we enjoy and pos-
> sess the holy fellowship and communion of the body and
> blood of Christ, by which our inward man is nourished and
> fed.[13]

The centred state of the worshippers can assist a distracted
mind. Even a single soul can serve as a midwife to the inward
birth of Christ in others whose minds are inattentive.[14] Such
ministry is anonymous, the recipients may simply feel
returned to the centre. At times, however, the whole meeting
may feel powerfully knit together. Friends call such an experience a 'gathered' or 'covered' meeting.[15] Thomas Kelly
(1893–1941) offered a description of this experience.

> In the Quaker practice of group worship on the basis of
> silence come special times when an electric hush and
> solemnity and depth of power steals over the worshipers.
> A blanket of divine covering comes over the room, a still-
> ness that can be felt is over all, and the worshipers are
> gathered into a unity and synthesis of life which is amaz-
> ing indeed. A quickening Presence pervades us, breaking
> down some part of the special privacy and isolation of our
> individual lives and blending our spirits within a
> superindividual Life and Power. An objective, dynamic
> Presence which enfolds us all, nourishes our souls, speaks
> glad, unutterable comfort within us, and quickens in us
> depths that had before been slumbering. The Burning
> Bush has been kindled in our midst, and we stand
> together on holy ground.[16]

Vocal Ministry

The utterance of words makes it clear even to an outside observer that Quaker meeting is a group experience. Quaker worship has been profitably compared with Buddhist forms of meditation.[17] An important difference is the focus on community in the Quaker tradition. Buddhist monks may gather in the meditation hall, but the goal is not a common experience.[18] If a meditator were suddenly to feel that she or he has a message to offer to the other meditators in the community, the urge to speak would be judged a distraction or illusion. As a group contemplative practice, Quaker meeting for worship has the group as its focus. In a Friends meeting for worship, the goal is not so much achieving individual enlightenment as ministering to the gathered body.

The motion to speak must come from a deep place, after sinking into the quiet centre where the boundaries of self begin to soften and the worshipper feels in communion with God and the worshipping community. The inward motion takes its origins there, below the level of consciousness where words have beginnings and endings, in the presence of a Word that was in the beginning. That motion rises through the soul's layers of awareness until words take form and a message takes shape. Although as Friends have experienced it, the water always tastes of the pipes, if the minister is faithful to the first motion, the words will still contain living water and will nourish the meeting. The minister does not so much speak as is spoken through, for the edification of those gathered.

The content of vocal ministry is unpredictable, though patterns have emerged. The minister may offer prayer. William Penn described George Fox at prayer in this touching portrait:

> But above all he excelled in prayer. The inwardness and weight of his spirit, the reverence and solemnity of his address and behaviour, and the fewness and fullness of his words, have often struck even strangers with admiration, as they used to reach others with consolation. The most awful, living, reverent frame that I ever felt or beheld, I

must say, was his in prayer. And truly it was a testimony that he knew and lived nearer to the Lord than other men.[19]

A minister at other times might feel that the group as a whole is centring down but not yet come collectively to the place of living water. Ministry at such a moment might be an exhortation to 'dwell deep', to come more fully into the inward sanctuary where God is met. Alternatively, a minister might simply offer words of Scripture, with or without additional commentary, for the community to hear and take into meditation.

The shape of vocal ministry has changed with the times. Rufus Jones spoke for the twentieth century:

> Vital ministry is not abstract and doctrinal, it is charged with insight for the meaning and significance of life. It answers back to specific human need. It 'speaks to the condition' of souls. It correlates with concrete reality. It sets hearts beating. It quickens drooping spirits. It restores waning faith. It fortifies the wills of those who hear it. It makes the world look different. That means that it must *come out of life* and, if it is to have value, it must refresh life.[20]

The story from Caroline Stephen recounted at the beginning of this chapter concurs. The words spoken in that first meeting for worship that she attended did not stay in her memory, but the inward place from which the words came did remain with her. They brought her peace; they 'came out of the life'.

To Speak or Not to Speak

Every freedom entails a proportionate risk. Quakers regard the ministry as free. It is open to all. Such a delicate form can be misled or abused. English Friend L. Violet Holdsworth, writing in 1919, put it in a delightfully blunt fashion:

> Each Friend who feels called upon to rise and deliver a lengthy discourse might question himself – and herself –

most searchingly as to whether the message could not be more lastingly given in the fewest possible words, or even through his or her personality alone, in entire and trustful silence. 'Cream always must rise to the surface.' True. But other substances rise to the surface besides cream; substances that may have to be skimmed off and thrown away before bodies and souls can be duly nourished. 'Is my message cream or scum?' may be an unusual and is certainly a very homely query. Still it is one that every speaker, in a crowded gathering especially, should honestly face. Some of the dangers of silent worship can be guarded against by its courtesies.[21]

The discernment to speak or not has several dimensions. If a worshipper feels a message from within, she or he must try the message to determine the source of the motion. One must practise self-vigilance, watchful of one's motives. The impulse to speak might come from a need for attention, or the urge to please others, or a desire to appear brilliant. Indulging a fragile ego and attempting to bolster a poor self-image result in messages that tire rather than edify the others present.

The urge to speak might also originate in the worshipper's passions for certain causes. Words rooted in these passions tend to burden others with a feeling of guilt. Meeting for worship is not the occasion for political persuasion. Again, it is not so much the substance of the message as the motion behind it. If the overriding theme is, 'If you love me, then you must love my cause', the motion is self-centred, aimed at serving the speaker rather than the rest of the community. Friends have ministered in prophetic words, calling for changed hearts and a changed society, as Lucretia Mott (1793–1880) did so well, but the motion was love for others rather than self-promotion.

Certainly God can work through our mixed motives, and vocal ministry may offer nourishment to some in the room despite its questionable origins. Friends have found it most helpful when careful discernment prevails. Then the ministry nourishes more of the community because it is rooted in the

God who gives life. The vitality is perceptible and contagious, whatever the words with which it clothes itself.

The next layer of discernment engages this question: For whom is the message intended? In the language of earlier Friends, a message may be meant to feed others or it may be 'bread for home', that is a revelation for the individual worshipper rather than the whole community. If the worshipper is able to stay centred in that prayerful place where she or he senses the gathered community, it is easier to answer that question.

After passing through these gates, the worshipper must still decide when to offer the message. Is this ministry meant for now? Friends have found that they can be given a word that is intended for another time. Or the ministry may be a genuine motion from God, but it serves the community better to pray it silently rather than to speak it aloud. The latter is another way in which a worshipper can be like a magnet, drawing the community closer through silent prayer, directed to the soul's true north.

Interior watchfulness must continue throughout the offering of vocal ministry in worship. Samuel Bownas (1676–1753) exhorted ministers, 'Keep close to thy gift . . . as thou beginnest with Spirit, keep to it in thy going on, and conclude in it.'[22] Otherwise one may 'outrun the Guide', as Friends put it. John Woolman (1722–72), in a compellingly honest self-disclosure, described such a moment. It was the first time he ventured to offer vocal ministry in meeting for worship. His reflections echo chapter John 10, where Jesus describes himself as the good shepherd, whose voice his sheep recognize. The sheep flee from the stranger, whose voice they do not know. To offer vocal ministry is an exercise in discerning the shepherd's voice.

> I went to meetings in an awful frame of mind and endeavoured to be inwardly acquainted with the language of the True Shepherd. And one day being under a strong exercise of spirit, I stood up and said some words in a meeting, but

not keeping close to the divine opening, I said more than was required of me.[23]

Aware of his failing, he was stricken for several weeks. When he finally felt led once again to speak in meeting, he stayed close to the Guide, which brought him peace. He reflected on this task of discernment:

> As I was thus humbled and disciplined under the cross, my understanding became more strengthened to distinguish the language of the pure Spirit which inwardly moves upon the heart and taught me to wait in silence sometimes many weeks together, until I felt that rise which prepares the creature to stand like a trumpet through which the Lord speaks to his flock.[24]

There is always the urge to go beyond the leading, to tidy things up, to make a strong finish – but this may be the task of the hearers to do in their own meditations, or of someone else who may feel called to speak. Since different worshippers may draw different conclusions from a spoken word, often the true leading may be to leave matters evocative and let God do the rest of the work in the heart of each worshipper. A seasoned Friend once advised me: 'The task is to get up when called, to speak as simply as possible, and then to *sit down*', to avoid outrunning the Guide.

Threshing Meetings

Over the centuries attitudes toward vocal ministry have swung back and forth. In the earliest years, meetings for worship could be quite lively if not altogether edifying events. In addition to Friends and sympathizers, a Quaker meeting attracted the curious and the furious. Sightseers came as though it were a side-show, hoping for something freakish. They might try to instigate something strange. Others came to debate and harangue. George Fox wrote of visits from hostile clergy who,

when they saw a hundred or two hundred people all silent,
waiting upon the Lord, they would break out into a won-
dering and despising, and some of them would say: 'Look
how these people sit mumming and dumming. What
edification is here where there are no words?' And they
said they never saw the like in their lives.[25]

The power of God nevertheless broke through in these meetings, despite the presence of 'the world's people'. A contempo-
raneous description of William Dewsbury's ministry offers a
view of early Quaker preaching:

In the latter end of the eighth month of the same year
[1652], William Dewsbury was moved to come into these
parts, and travelled much from town to town, sounding the
trumpet of the Lord. His testimony was piercing and very
powerful, so as the Earth shook before him, the mountain
did melt at the power of the Lord, which exceedingly, in a
wonderful manner, broke forth in these days in our holy
assemblies, to the rending of many hearts, and bringing
divers to witness the same state, measurably.[26]

Early Friends referred to these large public meetings as
'threshing meetings'. From these they would invite the reli-
giously earnest to attend smaller, private, more retired gather-
ings where the faithful could worship in relative peace, 'out of
the rude multitude', as Edward Burrough put it.[27] George Fox
attested to this distinction between worship among convinced
Friends and threshing meetings in his epistle addressed 'To
Quaker Ministers', written in 1652:

And when there are any meetings in unbroken places, ye
that go to minister to the world, take not the whole meeting of Friends with you thither, to suffer with and by the
world's spirit; but let Friends keep together and wait in
their own meeting-place: So will the life in the Truth be
preserved, and grow. And let three, or four, or six, that are
grown up and are strong in the Truth go to such unbroken

places, and thresh the heathenish nature; and there is true service for the Lord.[28]

The Swinging Pendulum

Decades of persecution turned Friends inward. By the eighteenth century, Quakers were on the whole no longer an unpredictable antisocial group in a topsy-turvy revolutionary age. Friends settled into a sectarian existence in an age of rationality and respectability. Meeting for worship was likewise more domesticated and predictable. Gone were the 'public threshings'. Propriety ruled the day, throughout England and the American colonies. Those who spoke in Quaker meeting tended to be those acknowledged by the community with a gift for ministry, the 'recorded' ministers. The self-confidence of early leaders gave way to relentless suspicion of the self. In worship, the silence became sacrosanct; some seemed almost to pride themselves on how many weeks or months went by with no speaking at all in their meetings. John Rutty's *Spiritual Diary* reports that in twenty-two successive meetings for worship in Dublin in 1770, vocal ministry was offered only a single time.[29] When the flock was not fed for so long a time, a decline in spiritual vitality resulted. In the nineteenth century this inspired some to look for inspiration from the lively and progressive movement of the era, the evangelical revival.

In the twentieth century, the tide turned again. Among many Friends, the practice of publicly acknowledging or 'recording' ministers was largely laid down, in the hopes that doing so would encourage all to be open to the possibility that they could be led to offer vocal ministry in worship. This has proven true, to a large extent, though some feel that the current openness has also resulted in a diminishment of the quality of speaking in worship. The awe that once accompanied the very thought of speaking in meeting has suffered something of a loss. While Friends at the present would not want to 'quench the Spirit' and discourage one another from being open to being led to speak, at the same time many desire a turning of the tide once again, toward more careful discernment about the call to minister in meeting.[30]

'The Still Life'

George Fox deserves the final word in this chapter on the meeting for worship. Though a vigorous preacher, he honoured the purpose of words, which is to take hearer beyond human utterance into the life and power of God. His words and imagery draw from the Song of Songs, where lover and beloved meet, and from the Gospel of John, where living bread and living water bring life to the faithful.

> Concerning silent meetings, the intent of all speaking is to bring into the life, and to walk in, and to possess the same, and to live in and enjoy it, and to feel God's presence, and that is in the silence . . . for there is the flock lying down at noon-day, and feeding of the bread of life, and drinking at the springs of life, when they do not speak words; for words declared are to bring people to it, and confessing God's goodness and love, as they are moved by the eternal Spirit . . . the still life, in which the fellowship is attained to in the Spirit of God, in the power of God, which is the Gospel, in which is the fellowship, where there are no words spoken.[31]

3. DISCERNMENT

The relationship between individuals and community has always been complex in Quakerism. The pendulum has swung back and forth in each chapter of Quaker history in an effort to avoid the extremes of anarchy and rigidity. There must be enough freedom so that the individual can be truly open to divine leadings because Friends hold that revelation is a continuing process, that God can lead people into new truths, especially in matters of ethics or morality. At the same time, there is a need for sufficient structure to preserve the tradition that has valued that freedom. Leadings come to individuals, but the group discerns whether they are genuine.

A community that emphasizes the present availability of divine guidance must take discernment seriously. Discernment is sorting, careful listening, and recognizing. Discernment offers tools to distinguish between an interior leading from God and an impulse whose origin is less worthy, such as a desire to feel important or look clever.

Friends practise communal discernment. Quakers have not established a code of rules for discernment, since they would suspect that such a code could straightjacket the Holy Spirit. Their historical practice of discernment suggests a number of tests for leadings.[1]

A leading is a motion from the Inner Light. It can be a movement to speak in meeting. Alternatively, it can be an urging to specific action outside of meeting for worship. John Woolman (1720–72), for example, felt a leading to travel to speak to slave-keepers to persuade them of the evils of holding other human beings in bondage. Lucretia Mott (1783–1880) felt led to advocate for the rights of women. Barbara Reynolds (1915–90) felt leadings to witness against the threat of the nuclear arms race.

Quaker historian Hugh Barbour identified four tests that early Friends came to develop to determine if a leading was Spirit-led. These tests grew out of the inward experience and the outward trials and tribulations of earliest Quakerism. These were not a checklist mechanically applied. They were more like signposts as one travelled down the path of a leading. As one lived attentively with the questions raised by these tests, they lent confidence that one was acting under divine guidance.

The first test was moral purity, though today we might say integrity. A God-given leading was not an impulse to mere self-indulgence. The era in which Quakerism arose saw all manner of religious experimentation. One rival group was known as the Ranters, who held that since they were redeemed no act was evil for them. Some Ranters consumed alcohol and tobacco in their worship services. Others granted themselves sexual license, or blasphemed publicly. Some Ranters were reported to have claimed that one was not free from a sin until one had committed it without feelings of guilt. Since opponents of Friends frequently accused them of Ranterism, early Quakers felt under strong obligation to be particularly clear for themselves and then describe to others how they discerned leadings.

Moral purity meant 'not fleeing the cross', referring to the moment in the Gospels when 'all the disciples abandoned him and fled' (see, for example, Matthew 26:56) as Jesus was arrested in Gethsemane. Not fleeing the cross meant obedience to leadings that were difficult and contrary to self-will. A contemporary example of fleeing the cross could be someone who announces to others that God is telling them to take risks that the speaker himself or herself is unwilling to take. A person who vociferously advocates getting arrested at, for example, a protest at the School of the Americas (a military institution in the United States justly notorious for its instruction in techniques of torture to agents of brutally repressive regimes in Latin America) yet fastidiously avoids arrest would be 'fleeing the cross'. A true leading demonstrates integrity; it does not make demands on others without expecting the same of the recipient of the leading.

The test of moral purity alone is not sufficient. This is especially so if it rests on a simplistic psychology that pits human will against divine will and posits that a leading is always contrary to one's self-will. At the extreme, a person could conclude that, because she or he would never want to engage in a particular action, precisely for that reason it must be the will of God. Such a position could lead one to some ridiculous behaviour. I, for example, have no interest in bungee-jumping off the Eiffel Tower, but I do not take that as an indication that therefore God obviously wants me to do so. In their youthful exuberance, some early Friends did perform some strange actions. A few, inspired by the prophet's example in Isaiah 20, went 'naked as a sign' to warn England of its moral nakedness.[2] Whatever the degree of the participants' nakedness, it was disturbing to their contemporaries, as Isaiah's was in his day. Some regard such symbolic action as a shock tactic in the Lamb's War, though it could also have served psychologically as a test of commitment to the group, perhaps like bizarre behaviours required for initiation into some secret societies. More generously, it may have served as training in an individual's humility. In any event, not fleeing the cross was insufficient as a test for a leading, as early Friends learned from the disastrous consequences of James Nayler's Palm Sunday-like ride into Bristol in 1656.[3]

A second test is patience. Put succinctly, 'self-will is impatient of tests'.[4] In an epistle to Friends in Barbados, George Fox wrote, 'Let all things be done in Love, and in the Spirit of Christ, which is the Spirit of the Lamb, that must have the Victory, for Patience runs the race and has the crown.'[5]

Traditionally Quakers speak of a leading being 'seasoned'. If God wills a particular course of action and reveals it at 10.30 on the first day of the week, if the leading is significant, God will continue to will it at 4.45 p.m., and the next day, and even weeks later. Divine will can outlast human impulse, so patience has been a useful test.

A third test rests on the conviction that the Holy Spirit is self-consistent. Early Friends resisted using the Scriptures as a manual or rule book, fearing that to do so might persuade some that direct experience of the Light is not necessary. Yet, because the Spirit that is present to the faithful to guide them is the same Spirit that gave forth the Scriptures, a biblical precedent to particular leading can confirm the Spirit's self-consistency.

Because of the firm belief in the self-consistency of the Spirit, Friends expected to be led into unity with one another as well as with biblical forebears. God would not lead the faithful into conflicting or contradictory actions. So the community itself was the locus of discernment. Early Friends would consult one another to discuss their leadings. As Quaker structures emerged, Friends who felt themselves 'under the weight of a concern' to travel in the ministry (such as those who felt led to visit slavekeepers to persuade them of the evils of slavery) would bring that concern to the community for discernment and endorsement. A hallmark of Quaker spirituality is the conviction that if the community is open to divine guidance, then unity will emerge. For this reason, divisions among Friends, such as the separations of the nineteenth century, have been especially painful. Still, today, when Quakers find themselves unable to unite upon a significant matter, it results in grief and anguish.

These tests largely focus on the content of a leading. Just as important are the inner dynamics of discernment. As with the tests, Quakers have been more inclined to show than to tell, and they reflect on these inward experiences in their religious autobiographies or journals. John Woolman, one of the most articulate and introspective of Quaker journalists, illustrates discernment in the tradition of Friends. John Woolman's life embraced many prophetic concerns, such as economic justice for the impoverished, abolishing slavery, maintaining peaceful relations with and justice for Native Americans, and refusal to pay war taxes. His *Journal* does not provide a checklist for mechanical assessment of leadings, but it does show us a sensitive soul in action. So what follows is not so much a set of guidelines as some observations drawn from a careful reading of John Woolman.

1. The raw material for a leading most often lies in ordinary life. We can find God there if we are attentive.

Life in a small town in the English colonies of North America required that most people have multiple talents to make ends meet. John Woolman was, among other things, a tailor, an orchard keeper, a school teacher, a surveyor, and a scrivener or writer of last wills and testaments and other legal documents. He had long been personally opposed to slavery, but his first public witness to that opposition came not in some extraordinary event but instead in the very ordinariness of daily life. He seems to have been caught off guard, but as he attended to the resulting affliction in his mind, he found that he was moved to deeper commitment.

> My employer, having a Negro woman, sold her and directed me to write a bill of sale, the man being waiting who bought her. The thing was sudden, and though the thoughts of writing an instrument of slavery for one of my fellow creatures felt uneasy, yet I remembered I was hired by the year, that it was my master who directed me to do it, and that it was an elderly man, a member of our society who bought her; so through weakness I gave way and wrote it, but at the executing it, I was so afflicted in my mind that I said before my master and the Friend that I believed slavekeeping to be a practice inconsistent with the Christian religion. This in some degree abated my uneasiness, yet as often as I reflected seriously upon it I thought I should have been clearer if I had desired to be excused from it as a thing against my conscience, for such it was.[6]

From this humble beginning of a meagre protest, a life direction was formed. When similar circumstances occurred later,

John Woolman declined to 'write an instrument of slavery', at times successfully convincing the slavekeeper to free the slaves. Throughout the rest of his life, he worked to end slave-keeping, particularly among Friends but also among other English colonists. His anti-slavery treatises bear the subtitle, 'Recommended to Professors of [that is, those who profess] Christianity of Every Denomination'.[7]

Historians of colonial America note that slavery was so interwoven in the fabric of everyday life as to be practically invisible – at least to those who were not slaves. It took unusual clear-sightedness to perceive how unjust it was and to imagine a society without slavery. John Woolman's vision was borne of keen attention to the ordinary details of life, to find God's presence and messages there.

2. A leading can begin in joy or sorrow, because either can be centred in love. John Woolman's story of his commitment to work against slavery and for human freedom began with a feeling of affliction, because he had been unfaithful to his convictions about human rights. He did not allow this feeling to push him into self-absorbed guilt; instead it drove him toward greater faithfulness. The important thing is the motion forward, not so much its origin. It moved him toward God.

John Woolman's *Journal* recounts his visit to the settlement of the Delaware nation at Wyalusing. The story began with his sense of leading to spend time among them:

> Having many years felt love in my heart toward the natives of this land who dwell far back in the wilderness, whose ancestors were the owners and possessors of the land where we dwell, and who for a very small consideration assigned their inheritance to us, and being at Philadelphia in the 8th month, 1761, on a visit to some Friends who had slaves, I fell in company with some of those natives who lived on the east branch of the river Susquehanna at an Indian town called Wyalusing, about two hundred miles from Philadelphia. And in conversation with them by an interpreter, as also by observations on

their countenance and conduct, I believed some of them were measurably acquainted with that divine power which subjects the rough and froward will of the creature; and at times I felt inward drawings toward a visit to that place, of which I told none except my dear wife until it came to some ripeness.[8]

He noted a mixture of feelings. The first was a concern for justice, based on the historical relations between the Delaware and the English colonists. The second was a joyful apprehension of a spiritual kinship with them and an anticipation of exploring that kinship. Both feelings were grounded in love. Even more important is the forward direction of a leading: a true leading moves toward greater love.

3. Beware of an apparent peace that is only superficial. The Holy Spirit can lead people in ways that are profoundly counter-cultural, particularly when the leading is to challenge injustice. There is a deep human yearning for community, but real community is centred in truth and in a love that does not deny the truth. Relationships and encounters that are less honest or that do not broach difficult subjects may be pleasant on the surface, but ultimately they are like 'false consolations' in other traditions. They draw us away from God. Feelings of superficial goodwill should not be misinterpreted as a sign that a leading is no longer valid. John Woolman's *Journal* records these reflections when he was travelling in the ministry, visiting slavekeepers in order to persuade them of the evils of slavery:

Thou who sometimes travels in the work of the ministry and art made very welcome by thy friends seest many tokens of their satisfaction in having thee for their guest. It's good for thee to dwell deep, that thou mayest feel and understand the spirits of people. If we believe Truth points toward a conference on some subjects in a private way, it's needful for us to take heed that their kindness, their freedom, and affability do not hinder us from the Lord's work. I have seen that in the midst of kindness and smooth conduct to speak close and home to them who entertain us, on points that relate to their outward interest, is hard labour . . .

To attempt to do the Lord's work in our own way and to speak of that which is the burden of the Word in a way easy to the natural part does not reach the bottom of the disorder. To see the failings of our friends and think hard of them, without opening that which we ought to open, and still carry a face of friendship – this tends to undermine the foundation of true unity. The office of a minister of Christ is weighty, and they who now go forth as watchmen had need to be steadily on their guard against the snares of prosperity and an outside friendship.[9]

On an occasion when John Woolman refused to write a will in which a slave was being bequeathed to an heir, he wrote:

In this case I had a fresh confirmation that acting contrary to present outward interest from a motive of divine love and in regard to truth and righteousness, and thereby incurring the resentments of people, opens the way to a treasure better than silver and to a friendship exceeding the friendship of men.[10]

Yet the inward resistance to be faithful can be considerable, resulting in lessons in humility. Here he took instruction from the prophet Jeremiah, with whom he identified in numerous ways.

Through the humbling dispensations of divine providence men are sometimes fitted for his service. The messages of the prophet Jeremiah were so disagreeable to the people and so reverse to the spirit they lived in that he became the object of their reproach and in the weakness of nature thought to desist from his prophetic office, but saith he: 'His word was in my heart as a burning fire shut up in my bones, and I was weary with forebearing and could not stay' [Jeremiah 20:9]. I saw at this time that if I was honest to declare that which Truth opened in me, I could not please all men, and laboured to be content in the way of my duty, however disagreeable to my own inclination.[11]

4. As we listen to divine guidance, our true desires are clarified. Central to discernment is discovering our deepest desires, where we are truly in tune with God's desires for humankind. The deepest human desire is to be loved and accepted by God, yet we so easily misdirect this desire and try to substitute mere wealth for genuine security in God, or worldly reputation and honour for acceptance with God, or social power for the experience of co-working with God's strength. As we 'attend to that Holy Spirit which sets right bounds to our desires',[12] we find our truest desire. Rather than renouncing power, wealth, and honour in a noble sacrifice, we simply discover that they no longer hold such interest for us. The dissatisfying substitute has yielded to the genuine substance.

5. Discernment requires ongoing vigilance. The direction of a leading may change as circumstances develop. John Woolman felt led to visit the Lenni Lenape settlement at Wyalusing but told no one but his family 'until it came to some ripeness'.[13] The ripeness did not come for over a year. He then brought the matter to his community for collective discernment and received their blessing, but by then relations between Native Americans and English colonists had deteriorated, in part because of dishonest practices by the English and in part because of the extension to the New World of the rivalries between the French and English monarchies. War was on the frontier, so travelling was perilous. John Woolman felt clear to continue, but only after much prayer and inward searching. 'In this conflict of spirit there were great searchings of heart and strong cries to the Lord that no motion might be in the least degree attended to but that of the pure spirit of Truth.'[14] After days of miserable weather, rough travelling, and poor sleeping conditions, he reflected on his motives, finding that love still lay at the centre, creating in him a willingness to learn from

those he was hoping to visit. The danger of war and uncomfortable travelling opened the way to empathy.

> It being a rainy day we continued in our tent, and here I was led to think on the nature of the exercise which hath attended me. Love was the first motion, and then a concern arose to spend some time with the Indians, that I might feel and understand their life and the spirit they live in, if haply I might receive some instruction from them, or they be in any degree helped forward by my following the leadings of Truth amongst them. And as it pleased the Lord to make way for my going at a time when the troubles of war were increasing, and when by reason of much wet weather travelling was more difficult than usual at that season, I looked upon it as a more favourable opportunity to season my mind and bring me into a nearer sympathy with them. And as mine eye was to the great Father of Mercies, humbly desiring to learn what his will was concerning me, I was made quiet and content.[15]

Yet vigilance was still required. As the danger to the lives of John Woolman and his companions increased, he once again turned inward.

> I thought that to all outward appearance it was dangerous travelling at this time, and was after a hard day's journey brought into a painful exercise at night, in which I had to trace back and feel over the steps I had taken from my first moving in the visit. And though I had to bewail some weakness which at times had attended me, yet I could not find that I had ever given way to wilful disobedience. And then as I believed I had under a sense of duty come thus far, I was now earnest in spirit beseeching the Lord to show me what I ought to do.
>
> In this great distress I grew jealous of myself, lest the desire of reputation as a man firmly settled to persevere through dangers, or the fear of disgrace arising on my

returning without performing the visit, might have some place in me. Thus I lay full of thoughts great part of the night, while my beloved companion lay and slept by me, till the Lord my gracious Father, who saw the conflicts of my soul, was pleased to give quietness. Then was I again strengthened to commit my life and all things relating thereto into his heavenly hands; and getting a little sleep toward day, when morning came we arose.[16]

John Woolman continued the journey, but on another occasion he did turn back. At that time it was not on account of danger but rather because he discerned that what motivated him to undertake the proposed journey was not a love that looks forward but instead a backward-looking guilt.[17] He had packed his provisions and was ready to embark, yet he was not afraid to return home when it became clear that this was his leading, even though such an action could be embarrassing. We must be willing to be led, moment by moment. Later he wrote:

Now I find that in pure obedience the mind learns contentment in appearing weak and foolish to that wisdom which is of the world; and in these lowly labours, they who stand in a low place, rightly exercised under the cross, will find nourishment. The gift is pure; and while the eye is single in attending thereto, the understanding is preserved clear; self is kept out; and we rejoice in filling up that which remains of the afflictions of Christ for his body's sake, which is the church ... A labour hath attended my mind, that the ministers amongst us may be preserved in the meek feeling life of Truth, where we have no desire but to follow Christ and be with him; that when he is under suffering we may suffer with him; and never desire to rise up in dominion, but as he by the virtue of his own Spirit may raise us.[18]

6. Discernment takes place in community. John Woolman submitted his leadings to travel in the ministry to his community. Travelling ministers would go forth in pairs, to check one

another's leadings. John Woolman found communities of support on controversial issues, such as war tax refusal, and he helped others to discern their leadings on such issues as well.[19]

7. A genuine leading will guide the way to action that 'appeals to the pure witness' in others, that is, to the witness of the Holy Spirit in others that confirms the truth of a matter. The Holy Spirit is persuasive, so such actions will be 'seasoned with charity'.

Some dramatic abolitionists, on the other hand, merely shocked and alienated those whom John Woolman hoped to convert. Benjamin Lay may serve as an example. An outrageous if committed abolitionist, he was eventually expelled or 'disowned' by Friends for his unusual efforts to dramatize the evils of slavery. During one Quaker gathering he rose to his feet and denounced slavekeepers. The cruelty of their slaveholding, he proclaimed, was as immoral as piercing the slaves' hearts with a sword. He then removed his plain Quaker greatcoat, revealing a military uniform. He unsheathed the sword and thrust it through a hollowed-out book, in which he had hidden a bladder of scarlet berry juice. The 'blood' splattered on those nearby. Some Friends perceived that, despite Benjamin Lay's passionate devotion to ending the evils of slavery, his motivations included drawing attention to himself and making a scene as much as they did concern to persuade others to change their views.[20]

A genuine leading would serve to change the hearts of slavekeepers, for example, not simply to anger them so that they would then have an excuse to stop listening. In John Woolman we see how the 'shock tactics' of the Lamb's War of the earliest period of Quakerism have given way to gentler but none the less persistent forms of changing the hearts of others.

8. Finally, discernment leads to a deep inner peace, despite any inconvenience on the mere surface. John Woolman described the feeling that follows carrying out a leading with expressions like these: 'peace', 'refreshment', 'inward calm and quiet',' heart enlarged' (to love others more fully), 'inward con-

solation'. Although he was 'united with the suffering seed', he 'found inward sweetness in these mortifying labours'.[21]

This inner peace, born of faithfulness, is of greater value than any particular result that follows upon acting on a leading:

> I have had renewed evidences that to be faithful to the Lord and content with his will concerning me is a most necessary and useful lesson for me to be learning, looking less at the effects of my labour than at the pure motion and reality of the concern as it arises from heavenly love. In the Lord Jehovah is everlasting strength, and as the mind by a humble resignation is united to him and we utter words from an inward knowledge that they arise from the heavenly spring, though our way may be difficult and require close attention to keep in it, and though the manner in which we may be led may tend to our own abasement, yet if we continue in patience and meekness, heavenly peace is the reward of our labours.[22]

Corporate Decision-making

Communal discernment shapes decision-making when Friends gather to do business. Just as in meeting for worship when Friends come into a powerful experience of unity, so they expect to come to unity when facing decisions. As a result, they do not decide by vote; they aspire to a unity deeper than majority rule. Edward Burroughs, writing in 1662, offered these guidelines for proceeding in a spirit of patience and love:

> Being orderly come together, [you are] not to spend your time with needless, unnecessary and fruitless discourses, but to proceed in the wisdom of God, not in the way of the world, as a worldly assembly of men, by hot contests, by seeking to outspeak and over-reach one another in discourse as if it were controversy between party and party of men, or two sides violently striving for dominion, not

deciding affairs by the greater vote, but in the wisdom, love, and fellowship of God, in gravity, patience, meekness, in unity and concord, submitting to one another in lowliness of heart, and in the holy Spirit of truth and righteousness all things [are] to be carried on; by hearing and determining every matter coming before you, in love, coolness, gentleness and dear unity – I say, as one only party, all for the truth of Christ, and for the carrying on the work of the Lord, as assisting one another in whatsoever ability God hath given; and to determine of things by a general mutual concord, in assenting together as one man in the spirit of truth and equity, and by the authority thereof.[23]

Because Friends place such a high value on unity, they are willing to wait until they can unite on a decision before moving ahead. Viewed from a merely secular point of view, this may seem impractical, not to mention exasperating in how long it seems to take to come to a decision. Even within a secular framework, however, this is not necessarily the case. If we imagine a line with 'idea' on one end and 'implementation' on the other, the distance between the two remains the same, no matter when the group chooses to make a decision. If the group settles on majority rule, the decision can come when just over half the group agrees to vote in the same way. We might chart it like this:

Idea -- Implementation

|

Decision

The distance from decision to implementation is still considerable. The majority may have to tow a significant minority, many of them dragging their feet, to the point of implementation. The losers feel defeated and may resist or even sabotage the practical policy resulting from the decision.

When all consent to the decision, however, we might chart the process like this:

Idea --- Implementation
                                    |
                                Decision

The distance from idea to decision seems immense, but once the decision is reached, the group may proceed directly to implementation. All can feel ownership of the process and of the decision. There are no disgruntled minorities determined to undermine the success of the policy. The group need not be divided into quarrelling factions. No one need feel compromised or marginalized. A stronger sense of community results.[24]

From a purely secular perspective, decision-making by consensus has obvious benefits. When the group is striving to discern the will of God, moreover, much more is at stake, and the rewards of faithful discernment are much deeper.

A Quaker meeting for business is sometimes called a meeting for worship with attention to business. Meeting for business begins in silent worship. As in meeting for worship, the silence is an opportunity to open oneself to the guiding hands of the Holy Spirit. It is not a time to organize one's thoughts or to devise the strategy of an argument to persuade others. If I have come with my mind made up, it is the time to 'unmake up' my mind, to feel my way into the centre, to encounter God on God's terms, which are always loving, even if they require that I set aside my personal predispositions. That quiet encounter with God can renew my faith in the collective wisdom of the community, when it also is grounded in God. Finding God's love in the silence awakens love for others in the room, and the community is ready to be led.

At the head of the meeting sits the residing officer, who has the humble title of 'clerk'. The clerk is the servant of the meeting. While the clerk arranges the agenda, recognizes those who wish to speak, and sets the pace of discussion, the clerk's chief task is to listen. She or he listens with a worshipful frame of mind, to assist the meeting in waiting for God's guidance. The clerk listens with discernment, encouraging the reticent to speak, since new insight may come from anyone. The meeting values the spoken contributions of those with greater experience but realizes as well that God may offer new truth through the young or the newcomer. The clerk may at times have to restrain the voices of those who speak at great length so that the community may hear from all quarters. The clerk herself or himself must at times exercise considerable self-restraint: as the one whose task is primarily to listen, the clerk must avoid advocating a particular opinion. If a matter arises in which the clerk discerns that her or his own predilections obscure the ability to read the sense of the meeting, the clerk should stand aside and request that the meeting appoint someone else to serve as clerk while that particular matter is under consideration.

The clerk's primary duty is to discern the 'sense of the meeting'. When it seems clear from discussion that the community is ready to move ahead in unity on a particular matter, the clerk seeks to articulate that unity in a minute. The clerk then tests that unity with the meeting. She or he may say something like this: 'Friends appear united (on such and such a decision). Are Friends ready to approve (such and such a proposal)?' If those present agree, usually with an expression such as 'I approve' or 'I unite with that', then the meeting moves on to the next item for consideration. Discerning both the sense of the meeting and the moment to articulate it, without the group feeling rushed or wearied into submission, is a spiritual gift, but it comes after listening deeply and attentively.

Unity does not always come easily; at times it does not come at all. When a community is in disagreement, it is often an opportunity for self-examination by all present: How has each sought to determine God's will? How successfully has each person set aside personal preferences, to be open to divine guidance? Have all attempted to give sympathetic consideration to the viewpoint of those with whom they disagree? What elements of truth might there be in the differing perspectives? Where is love?[25]

In moments of conflict, the clerk may ask those present to return in a focused way to silent worship. In the humility and vulnerability that worship requires, emotional attachments to particular positions can soften. The community can re-gather its centeredness in God's love and be reawakened to its spiritual bonds to one another. The Light can expose arrogance or stubbornness masquerading as leadings.

Similarly, the Spirit can affirm genuine leadings, even when these seem to run counter to the leanings of the apparent majority. Friends are sensitive to this, remembering that abolitionists, at first a minority, perceived the truth about slavery before the rest of the community. Some abolitionists withdrew from Friends, impatient with the others' resistance to the radical demands of the gospel. Others like John Woolman endured, maintaining faithfulness both to their leading and to their community, waiting until the rest could join them, and committed both to redeeming slaves from slavery and slaveholders from their mistaken views.

It can happen during a business meeting that a few may continue to hold reservations about a proposal. They may not feel unity of mind with the meeting, though they may find unity of heart. Having stated their objection, they may say, 'I do not wish to stand in the way of the meeting', allowing the community to move ahead, but with some humility. Standing aside in this way affirms unity with the community and obliges those who do so to accept the decision of which they have been a part.

On very rare occasions, rightly or wrongly, someone will say, 'I cannot unite with the proposed action', and feel unable to stand aside. When a person 'stands in the way', the meeting cannot move forward. The clerk may ask that all return to the topic on another occasion. In the meantime, all are expected to examine their souls. Some Friends who are recognized as spiritually sensitive may be asked to meet with those who are out of unity, to search the matter more deeply.

The following story from Elwood Cronk shows communal discernment at work:

> Most Friends understand that the sense of the meeting does not necessarily mean 100 percent approval. However, it does mean that Friends are in unity. Unity is a far stronger definition than 'general agreement' or 'solidarity in sentiment and belief'. The sense of the meeting means that, while some Friends may not be in full agreement regarding a proposed course of action, they are willing for the meeting to move forward.
>
> The concept was seldom more dramatically exemplified than at an early meeting of the American Friends Service Committee. Portions of several days were spent in discussing a proposed new program. Each time the matter was discussed, a Friend spoke against the involvement of the AFSC. Finally, Rufus Jones, who was presiding, said, 'Friend, we have listened to your views and feelings about this matter. Yet it is clearly the sense of the meeting that we approve the program. Are you willing to stand aside in view of the desire of the meeting to move forward?' The response was 'yes', and when the meeting concluded, the man came forward and said, 'Rufus, it's going to take money to start this program. Here's my check.' There was clearly more than 'general agreement' at work in this meeting! The profound difference is that unity was sought in a meeting for worship in which business affairs were conducted. In the search for unity, the group was sensitive to the leadings of the Spirit as it sought to discern its movement in the life of the gathered meeting.[26]

To conclude, Quakers have found that communal discernment brings them into unity with God and one another. When genuinely open to the guidance of God, we can discover a way forward that is superior to any previously held opinion that any one of us brought into the room. When we succeed in getting in touch with our own deepest desires, instead of our surface desires that can be a distortion or digression from the deeper desires, we find that those deep desires are in fact what God desires. For Friends, those deep desires can often be articulated in terms of our testimonies of equality, simplicity, integrity, and peace. Or they might be expressed in the apostle Paul's famous triad of faith, hope, and love. Because those deep desires come from God, they can draw us into unity and into clarity.

Clearness Committees: A Tool for Discernment

A recent development among Friends has been the use of a clearness committee as a tool for discernment. The historical antecedent was a committee to determine whether a couple was ready for marriage. In earlier times, the committee would meet with the couple to see that they were 'clear' of other obligations and therefore free to take up married life together. As time went on, the committee took on a more explicitly pastoral role, meeting with the couple in worship, asking gentle but provoking questions, offering thoughtful advice, and listening to the couple to hear how ready they were in terms of personal maturity to begin the blessings and challenges of life together. A spunky member of my marriage clearness committee bluntly asked, 'What do you argue about? Who wins, and why?' That question alone has seen us through numerous difficult moments over the years and invited us to see ourselves anew.

In the twentieth century, Friends extended this use of clearness committees, adapting this form to assist people to discern leadings in many areas of their lives.[27] Many Quakers and other-than-Quakers have found the clearness committee a useful tool, so it deserves a place in an introductory book on Quaker spirituality.

When a person faces a significant decision, she or he may choose to gather a group of four to six others. Ideally, they should be seasoned listeners, people with experience in attention to the subtle movements of the Spirit. Many find that a truly diverse committee works best, since then there is the most life experience to draw on. One person serves as clerk, whose task is to be observant of the process itself, to announce moments of transition, and to remind others, if needed, of the guidelines. Another serves as recording clerk, so that the person in focus can have a record of the process that can aid in further discernment. Neither task prevents asking questions of the person seeking clearness.

Often it is helpful if the person gathering the committee can circulate in advance a written statement describing the issue to be discussed, along with pertinent background information. To do so helps not only the other committee members but also helps to clarify the matter for the person seeking clearness.

The meeting begins in silent worship. The committee holds up the focal person in prayer, whether spoken or not, and a prayerful attitude prevails throughout the gathering. This worshipful stance, however, need not be glum. As any reader of Scripture or observer of the created world knows, God surely has a sense of humour, so prayerfulness does not preclude playfulness. A loving attention can be seasoned with laughter.

When ready, the person in focus begins with a summary of the issue at hand. The committee is then free to ask questions. Like good spiritual direction, their questions are invitations for the person in focus to turn inward, to listen to God for the deeper responses. Questions should grow out of a loving listening. They may not be sermons in disguise or advice cloaked in the interrogative. The committee has no answers that can fix things for the person seeking clearness. For the inexperienced, abstaining from offering advice can be an enormous demand. It can also require great self-discipline not to ask questions that chiefly indulge a committee member's curiosity. By listening intently, both to the person seeking clearness as well as to the Spirit of God who is in their midst, committee members can find themselves asking the most useful questions. At times they may find themselves asking intuitive, out-of-the-blue questions that can invite the person in focus to a deeper level.

It is essential to be comfortable with silence. The person seeking clearness needs time to absorb the questions and to reflect. A supportive pause before asking another question respects and weighs the previous response. The person in focus is always free not to answer a question – it may be a question that is too private for the moment, or one that needs to be lived with for a time before responding.

Toward the end of the time together, some find it useful if committee members have an opportunity to reflect back on what they have heard. Again, it is not a time to offer suggestions but rather to note recurrent themes or responses that seemed significant. If so led, the clerk may offer a kind of summary statement before the group returns to silent worship to close the gathering.

In recent years non-Quakers, including members of the Jesuit and Benedictine communities, have looked to Friends for new insights into communal discernment and decision-making.[28] As is shown by the increasing popularity of clearness committees outside Quaker circles, these methods are available to any who open themselves to the Spirit of God. Our hyper-individualistic era can benefit from a wider renewal of collective discernment.

4. NURTURING THE INWARD LIFE

Like the Eucharist for Roman Catholics, meeting for worship is central for Quaker spirituality but is not the whole of the spiritual life. Friends have developed and encouraged other practices to nurture the inward life. This chapter surveys several of them: interior prayer, epistles, meditative reading of Scripture, travelling ministry, spiritual nurture by elders, and advices and queries.

Interior Prayer

Meeting for worship is a corporate experience, and it must be complemented by nourishment of the individual in times of 'retirement' given to private devotions. Books of discipline query the reader: 'Do you nurture your spiritual life with prayer and silent waiting and in the regular study of the Bible and other devotional literature?'[1] Quakers have practised many forms of prayer, generally taking their inspiration from the apostle Paul, 'we do not know how to pray as we ought, but that very Spirit intercedes with sighs too deep for words' (Romans 8:26). Though they have read Scripture prayerfully and found sustenance in the Psalms and other prayers of the Bible, Friends have preferred spontaneous rather than composed prayer in their intercessions, confessions, praise, and thanksgiving.

A Guide to True Peace

Two writings on prayer have been especially influential among Friends.

The first, entitled *A Guide to True Peace, Or The Excellency of Inward and Spiritual Prayer*, was edited anonymously by William Backhouse and James Janson in 1813. The little book has passed through many printings ever since. This brief manual on prayer was drawn from the works of three European writers: Madame Guyon, François Fénelon, and Miguel de Molinos.[2] All three writers were active in the late 1600s and were well received at first on the continent. Molinos' early supporters reportedly included Pope Innocent XI and even censors of the Inquisition. All three writers eventually fell from favour and faced charges of heresy, complicated by ecclesiastical politics and rivalries. Their influence among Friends preceded the compilation assembled in 1813. Quaker James Gough had anonymously translated works by all three writers in the late 1700s. Sarah Lynes Grubb wrote of efforts to learn French in mid-life in order to read Guyon and Fénelon in the original.[3] The *Guide to True Peace*, which remains in print to this day, strengthened and perpetuated the influence of these continental mystics on Friends.[4]

William Backhouse and James Janson wrote of their work: 'it has been thought necessary to simplify, and render more intelligible, some of their terms, in order that they may be more generally understood.'[5]

The goal of the *Guide* is to teach 'a species of prayer which may be exercised at all times, which doth not obstruct outward employments, and which may be equally practiced by all ranks and conditions of people'.[6] In order to be suitable to all sorts, it must be a form of prayer not 'of the head, but of the heart'.[7] It is a prayer 'of inward silence, wherein the soul, abstracted from all outward things, in holy stillness, humble reverence, and lively faith, waits patiently to feel the Divine presence, and to receive the precious influence of the Holy Spirit.'[8]

Although this form of prayer is applicable under all circumstances, it can also be practised in specific times of 'retirement'. The method for the latter occasions is this: 'Consider yourselves as being placed in the Divine presence', looking intently to God and resigned to receive whatever God may give. At the same time, 'fix your minds in peace and silence; quitting all your own reasons, and not willingly thinking on any thing', no matter how good it may seem. If distractions occur, simply turn gently from them and wait in patience to feel God's presence.[9]

The *Guide* advises its readers to pray in equanimity, 'not that ye may enjoy spiritual delights, but that ye may be full or empty, just as it pleaseth God'[10] – for 'inquietude is the door by which the enemy gets into the soul, to rob it of its peace'.[11] Disinterested love of God characterizes true prayer.

If 'something of inward stillness, or a degree of the softening of the Divine Spirit, is mercifully granted', appreciate it, be attentive to it, but do not fan your own flames in an effort to heighten the experience. Echoing Robert Barclay's words on meeting for worship, the *Guide* describes this 'prayer of inward silence' as 'the most secure, because it is abstracted from the operations of the imagination'.[12] Like early monastic writers or the Spanish Carmelite reformers, the *Guide* (and Robert Barclay) subscribe to a psychology that holds that demons can only enter the soul through the senses. To abstain from sensory data is to deny evil access to the soul.

Wonderful experiences and sweet consolations are delightful, but they are not the purpose. Genuine prayer is the act itself, the attentive desire, the patient gaze God-ward, not fleeting moments of pleasure: 'True prayer consists, not in enjoying the light, and having knowledge of spiritual things, but in enduring with patience, and persevering in faith and silence; believing that we are in the Lord's presence, turning to him in our hearts with tranquillity and simplicity of mind.'[13]

Seeking consolations through self-exertion leads to deception. Those who pray must learn to discern such fabricated 'meltings of the affections from the operations which purely proceed from the Divine Spirit.'[14]

This little manual of prayer speaks of union of the soul with God through 'death of self', 'resignation', 'surrender of your will to the divine will', 'submission to the cross', and 'annihilation', but the soul is not to make itself dead but rather to become as receptive as it can to God's work within it.[15]

More recent works on prayer make a distinction between ceaseless prayer, which uses a mantra amid all waking activities, and modes of interior prayer such as centring prayer.[16] In the former, a phrase is repeated to bring one into mindfulness of God in all of life, reshaping all action into a conscious prayerfulness. The goal here is to remember the words of the prayer as much as possible, to maintain an awareness of divine presence. In the latter, a phrase or image is used in a focused way, in a time set aside for prayer alone. In this kind of interior prayer, the goal is ultimately to move beyond the words of the prayer into an apprehension of God's presence at a level that is deeper than the discursive power of the mind. Because of this distinction, some contemporary proponents of these methods of prayer suggest that the phrases chosen for each kind of prayer should be different so that one maintains an awareness of the different purposes of these two ways of praying.

The *Guide to True Peace* seems to combine these two modes of prayer, suggesting that this form of prayer can function both as a constant background in all occasions and as a concentrated, focused contemplative practice. The *Guide* differs from contemporary methods, though, in that in either mode of prayer, the content is imageless and wordless. The *Guide* invites its readers to raise background prayer to a more fully apophatic practice.

A Testament of Devotion

The second Quaker text on prayer is *A Testament of Devotion*, a collection of essays by Thomas R. Kelly, published posthumously after his sudden death, edited by his friend and colleague Douglas V. Steere, himself a significant voice in the history of Quaker spirituality. Thomas Kelly wrote with a freshness, a passion, and at times almost an ecstasy, that speaks to contemporary ears. He was a learned philosopher, educated in the thought of Meister Eckhart, Alfred North Whitehead, and classical Buddhism, yet he could speak with the simplicity of Brother Lawrence of the Resurrection, a humble Carmelite friar of seventeenth-century France, whom he admired highly.

> There is a way of ordering our mental life on more than one level at once. On one level we may be thinking, discussing, seeing, calculating, meeting all the demands of external affairs. But deep within, behind the scenes, at a profounder level, we may also be in prayer and adoration, song and worship and a gentle receptiveness to divine breathings.[17]

Thomas Kelly's focus was on ceaseless prayer rather than focused times of prayer. He described this interior form of prayer in apt metaphors that have won the hearts of many readers.

> What is here urged are internal . . . habits of unceasing orientation of the deeps of our being about the Inward Light, ways of conducting our inward life so that we are perpetually bowed in worship, while we are also very busy in the world of daily affairs . . . He who is within us urges, by secret persuasion, to such an amazing Inward Life with Him, so that, firmly cleaving to Him, we always look out upon all the world through the sheen of the Inward Light, and react toward men spontaneously and joyously from this Inward Center.[18]

Erudite philosopher though he was, Thomas Kelly could employ unabashedly the rhetoric of the passionate preacher in his invitation to take up the practice of this form of prayer.

> How, then, shall we lay hold of that Life and Power, and live the life of prayer without ceasing? . . . Begin now, as you read these words, as you sit in your chair, to offer your whole selves, utterly and in joyful abandon, in quiet,

glad surrender to Him who is within . . . Walk and talk and work and laugh with your friends. But behind the scenes, keep up the life of simple prayer and inward worship.[19]

The form of the prayer is at first verbal. Thomas Kelly recommended simple phrases, such as a fragment from the Psalms, heartfelt outbursts such as 'My God, my God, my Holy One, my Love', or the ecstatic cry of the Upanishads, 'O Wonderful, O Wonderful, O Wonderful'.[20] But words may give way to 'wordless attitudes of adoration'. When one becomes aware of lapses of attention, the task is simply to return to the verbal form of prayer, 'lose no time in self-recriminations'.[21] With practice, what begins as alternation of attention between prayer and outward action may grow into 'simultaneity':

> The first signs of simultaneity are given when at the moment of recovery from a period of forgetting there is a certain sense that we have not completely forgotten Him. It is as though we are only coming back onto a state of vividness which had endured in dim and tenuous form throughout . . . Again, it is like waking from sleep yet knowing, not by inference but by immediate awareness, that we have lived even when we were asleep.[22]

If a person outside the Society of Friends has read a single work of Quaker spirituality from the twentieth century, it is likely to have been Thomas Kelly's *Testament of Devotion*, which has remained in print since its first appearance in 1941, shortly after Thomas Kelly's untimely death.[23]

Epistles

As with the early Church, epistles have always served to strengthen bonds of community among Friends. Quakerism arose in a polemical age, and so many early writings are responses to external attacks and have a defensive tone.

Letters among Friends, however, breathe a more pastoral air. They offer guidance and support. As in other Christian traditions, letters impart instruction in spiritual formation.[24] As usual, early Friends were suspicious of formal methods, since these could quench the Spirit and become a substitute for direct experience of the Light. Yet the spiritual advice that letters contain offer concrete hints as to the outlines of spiritual disciplines.

In the following epistle written by George Fox in 1652, we can see the broad outlines of a spiritual practice. The letter warns its readers that temptation comes through habits and compulsions, that is, in places where human freedom is already held captive. These are our weakest places internally, since we have already to a degree renounced our power to act freely. George Fox invites his readers to be still 'in that which is pure', to be calm in the presence of the Light, not to exhaust oneself in fighting the temptation but rather to allow God to do the work. Then the strength of God comes, which brings peace.

> Friends: Whatever you are addicted to, the tempter will come to you in that thing; and when he can trouble you, then he gets advantage over you, and then you are gone. Stand still in that which is pure, after you see yourselves, and then mercy comes in. After thou seest thy thoughts and thy temptations, do not think but submit; and then the power comes . . . Stand still in the Light and submit to it, . . . sink down in that which is pure, and all will be hushed, and fly away . . . and then strength comes from the Lord, and help, contrary to your expectation. Then ye grow up in peace and no trouble shall move you.[25]

If there is a method to be drawn from this, it might be phrased in this way. Temptation comes to us at our most defenceless points, where we have the least power to resist. So sink into the presence of the Light, and permit God to engage the struggle. This letting go renders us available to the power of God, even though our instinct is to fight the temptation on our own. Stand still and attend to the Light that reveals our weakness and lends us strength. Then inner peace will arrive.

George Fox wrote a letter to Elizabeth Claypole, the daughter of Oliver Cromwell, who was suffering emotionally. His words suggest a similar strategy. Dwelling on our weakness and sinfulness can absorb us in depression. Focusing instead on that Light that reveals them, we open ourselves to the power of God and the way to peace.

> Be still and cool in thy own mind and spirit from thy own thoughts, and then thou wilt feel the principle of God to turn thy mind to the Lord God, whereby thou wilt receive his strength and power from whence life comes, to allay all tempests, against blusterings and storms . . . Looking down at sin, and corruption, and distraction, you are swallowed up in it; but looking at the light that discovers them, you will see over them. That will give victory; and you will find grace and strength; and there is the first step of peace.[26]

James Nayler, before his disastrous ride into Bristol in 1656, was a leading Quaker, arguably the equal of George Fox. The following letter, written from Appleby prison in 1653, displays the salient features of his spirituality. Like other Quaker writings, it is filled to the brim with scriptural allusions, especially Romans, Hebrews, and the Song of Songs. Words of spiritual consolation abound in this epistle: love, joy, freedom, rest, life. James Nayler is sceptical of the 'world', a place of sin, death, and inappropriate pleasures. The path of Christ, therefore, is a path of the cross. At the end of this path lies rest and glory, but it passes through shame and suffering. The world will despise us as it despised Jesus. Finally, James Nayler's eschatological tone is evident: the hour is now. Arise from the dead, the day of deliverance is at hand. The inward resurrection and eternal life stand at the door.

My dear hearts, whom the Lord hath manifested so much love unto, as to call you out of sin and death, and the world, . . . up to himself, where is joy unspeakable, pleasures and riches that endure for evermore. Dear friends, watch and be sober, that you may hear the voice of your beloved when he calleth; . . . the Lord of Sabbaths, who is your rest, and he is now appeared to deliver you, and set you free from bondage, that you may serve him alone, . . . follow your captain, the Lord Jesus Christ, who . . . endured the cross, despised the shame, and so entered into rest and glory . . . Mind your guide and follow him. Arise, shine, your light is come and the glory of the Lord is come upon you, the night is far spent, the day is at hand, even the day of Sion's deliverance; Arise come away, all you that love her, . . . Awake, thou that sleepest, and stand up from the dead, that Christ may give thee light. Come forth, come forth of all created things . . . This is the day of your deliverance . . . Rejoice, rejoice, ye meek of the earth, shout for joy, ye despised ones.[27]

This epistle offers less of a specific spiritual method than the letter of George Fox, yet as an invitation to spiritual transformation it is a powerful call to heed the inward availability of the reign of God. Like Sarah Blackborrow, whom we met above, James Nayler blended realized eschatology with the blissful love of the Song of Songs, long a favourite of mystics in both church and synagogue.

Letters from later periods in Quaker history also offer a kind of spiritual direction. As in the following excerpt from a letter from Richard Shackleton in 1772, counsel can be very personal, directed at the particulars of the recipient's life rather than a general admonition to all conditions. Writing in the late 1700s, when Friends were tempted to overemphasize mere external conformity to the trappings of Quaker culture, Richard Shackleton advised John Conran not to copy the example of his contemporaries but instead to be open to the fresh and possibly surprising leadings of God.

I have no doubt but that, as thy letter very sensibly inti-
mates, the first great work of the inward creation has
been, in measure, effected in thee, and the great first
moving Cause to every right and religious sense, has
said, 'Let there be light.' . . . Well, dear friend, keep to this
light, and walk in the shinings of it, and thereby thou
wilt know, in the progress of this inward work, . . .
Religion consists in knowledge and practice, hearing
Christ's sayings and doing them. Our great duty then is,
diligently to wait on the motions of his Spirit in our own
hearts, and faithfully to obey its requirings . . . We may
be clear in the head, and yet deceived in the heart . . . Let
us, therefore, my dear friend, walk cautiously and cir-
cumspectly as in the day . . . waiting patiently to be fed in
due season, . . . not seeking to be any thing in form or
degree, but as the inward operative principle of Life shall
gradually make us. The inward, as well as the outward
creation is . . . infinite in its variety. Let us, therefore, not
be so solicitous to model our conduct after the example of
others, as desirous in simplicity to be what the Lord
would have us to be. If we are passive enough in his hand
to be squared, fashioned and fitted by him, there is no
fear, but, that in due time, he will bring us into our proper
respective places in the spiritual building, in his church.[28]

Meditative Reading of Scripture

The abundance of biblical images in the letter above from
James Nayler shows another feature of early Quaker spirituality. Early Quaker epistles reveal a meditative way of reading Scripture, similar to the medieval monastic practice of
sacred reading or *lectio divina*. Once again, early Quakers
were more prone to show than to tell. The abundance of biblical allusions in early Quaker literature points to a spiritual
mentality sensitive to the poetic qualities of biblical images
and open to meditating on those images in a free-associative
manner worthy of a twelfth-century Cistercian.

The following extract from a letter from George Fox may serve as an example. He wrote it in 1663, a time of severe persecution for Friends. The exact recipients of this epistle remain unknown, but it is safe to assume that they were under great trials for their faith. This was the era of the Clarendon Code, a group of laws designed to render groups like Quakers extinct. As Friends were filling the English jails, George Fox wrote these words of encouragement:

> Sing and rejoice, you children of the Day and of the Light. For the Lord is at work in this thick night of darkness that may be felt. Truth does flourish as the rose, the lilies do grow among the thorns, the plants a-top of the hills, and upon them the lambs do skip and play.[29]

Less than sixty words in length, this passages overflows with biblical references. Identifying the sources of his scriptural images opens a layeredness of meaning to this proclamation of consolation.

'Sing and rejoice' is an echo from Zechariah 2:10: 'Sing and rejoice, O daughter Zion! For lo, I will come and dwell in your midst, says the Lord.' The wider context of 'Sing and rejoice' is a declaration of hope and restoration. Before Zechariah's time, the Babylonian empire had conquered Jerusalem and led many of its citizens into captivity. Zechariah addresses the exiles in Babylon, urging them to 'escape to Zion'. To those still suffering the effects of the Babylonian captivity, the prophet promises restoration and divine presence. The recipients of this letter from George Fox were invited to identify with those singing, rejoicing returnees. Even while still in prison, they could know the presence of the God who dwelt within them.

The phrase 'you children of the Day and of the Light' originates from 1 Thessalonians 5:5 and reflects the centrality of the Light in early Quaker experience, the divine beacon that first showed with all its terrifying power human sinfulness and then led to a sense of victory, peace, and community. In the epistle, 'Light', like 'Day', contrasts with night in the following sentence.

'For the Lord is at work in this thick night of darkness that may be felt' refers to Exodus 10:21, where God told Moses to stretch out his hand toward the heavens 'so that there may be darkness over the land of Egypt, a darkness that can be felt'. This darkness is one of the ten plagues of Egypt, a darkness so thick as to be palpable, but the children of Israel were spared. As with the call to rejoice because the exile is over, this was a message of comfort and hope. Despite the literal darkness of the prisons, like the ancient Israelites, Friends had the Light with them.

'Truth does flourish as the rose, the lilies do grow among the thorns' weaves together two biblical sources: Isaiah 35:1, which proclaims that 'The wilderness and the dry land shall be glad, the desert shall rejoice and blossom like the rose' (Authorized Version), and the Song of Songs 2:1, 'I am a rose of Sharon, a lily of the valleys.' The passage from Isaiah, like the previous text from Zechariah, was written to encourage the exiles. A vast desert lay between Babylon, the site of captivity, and Zion, where God had chosen particularly to dwell. Isaiah not only promised return to the homeland, but also proclaimed that even the journey itself would be full of wonders. The desert would bloom and, as Zechariah commanded the daughter of Zion, would sing and rejoice. Here again lay hope for the exiles, a promise of restoration and renewed life for those who were suffering.

The Song of Songs was for many centuries interpreted as a celebration of the love between God and the believer, favoured by mystics for describing an intimate experience of unity with God. So with these few words, George Fox suggested both deliverance and the intense presence of God, the soul's beloved.

The phrase 'the plants a-top of the hills' echoes the prophet Jeremiah's response to the suffering that followed the Babylonian conquest of Jerusalem. As Judah lay in ruins and the exiles were marched into captivity, Jeremiah proclaimed consolation: 'I have loved you with an everlasting love; therefore I have continued my faithfulness to you. Again I will build you, . . . Again you shall plant vineyards on the mountains of Samaria; the planters shall plant, and shall enjoy the fruit' (Jeremiah 31:3-5).

In the final phrase, 'and upon them the lambs do skip and play', lies another double reference. The first is to Psalm 114, which retells the story of the Exodus, the escape from bondage in Egypt. The Exodus and the crossing of the Jordan River into the Promised Land after the forty years of wandering in the wilderness are seen almost as a single event, as two aspects of God's redeeming activity. Psalm 114 celebrates the natural wonders of the events: creation itself affirms God's work in freeing the chosen people and bringing them into a homeland: 'When Israel went out from Egypt, . . . The sea looked and fled; Jordan turned back. The mountains skipped like rams, the hills like lambs' (vv. 1, 3-4). Like the psalmist, George Fox had a fondness for the natural world and drew on it for metaphors for the inward life.

The second text echoed here is, once again, the Song of Songs: 'The voice of my beloved! Look, he comes, leaping upon the mountains, bounding over the hills' (2:8). With a few strokes, George Fox has hinted both of God's deliverance in times of persecution and of God's loving intimacy.

So beneath the surface of this letter lies a deeper message of comfort to a persecuted people – repeated references to hope for deliverance from bondage, for a return to freedom, reminders of the intimate, intense presence of God despite their times of suffering.

It is images rather than rational argument that organize this mosaic of biblical allusions. The choice of biblical texts, however, was deliberate, so that the reader might reflect on the wider context of each allusion. Such a use of Scripture is based on a meditative way of reading, allowing the imagery from each passage to comment upon and deepen the meaning of the next. Scripture animated the world of early Friends. To read in this manner was to invite the Spirit who gave forth the Scriptures to reflect in the mirror of the reader's life.

Journals

Quotations from journals have appeared in this book from the first pages, underscoring how central they have been to Quakerism from the earliest days. Given the inwardness of Quaker spirituality, the reflective nature of journal keeping is a natural fit for Friends. Early Quakers learned how to write journals from their Puritan contemporaries, who followed a typical scheme of childhood intimacy with God, followed by a period of waywardness, then a conversion, a call to the ministry, and an account of one's work in the ministry. Friends adapted this basic pattern, though the conversion became a convincement of and commitment to the particulars of Quaker belief and practice.[30] Any pattern can become dull and formulaic, and some Quaker journals read like travelogues with a sprinkling of platitudes and Quaker jargon. But the best of Quaker journals are fresh in insight and arresting in their degree of self-honesty.

Suffering

Some contain moving accounts of suffering for religious conviction, such as the account of Elizabeth Stirredge (1634–1706), who lived through the fiercest persecutions under the Conventicle Act, which prohibited worship that did not follow the Anglican *Book of Common Prayer*.[31] Katharine Evans and Sarah Cheevers' journal recounted their imprisonment and sufferings at the hands of the Inquisition.[32] Readers must have drawn strength and encouragement from the commitment of these Friends, long after the time of the events recorded. Friends suffering for their pacifist position in the twentieth century, for example, found inspiration in the Civil War diary of Cyrus Pringle (1838–1911), who underwent torture and repeated threat of death for his refusal to bear arms in the 1860s.[33]

Other journals illustrate a quality of reflection that invite readers to do the same. John Woolman's inward struggles toward discernment, described in an earlier chapter, can invoke a comparable honesty and interior watchfulness from attentive readers.

Dreams and Visions

Quaker journalists recorded dreams that they deemed significant, acknowledging that dreams are one possible path of divine communication.

Elizabeth Ashbridge, before becoming a Quaker, was despairing and considering suicide to escape from her miserable condition as an indentured servant. She found solace when she dreamed of 'a grave woman, holding in her right hand a lamp burning, who said, "I am sent to tell thee that, if thou wilt return to the Lord thy God, who created thee, he will have mercy on thee, and thy lamp shall not be put out in obscurity." Her lamp then flamed in an extraordinary manner.'[34] This encouraging dream lent strength to Elizabeth Ashbridge, enabling her to endure.

Mary Penington, during her period of religious seeking and before she encountered Friends, recorded a dream in which Christ had come, accompanied by his bride, the Lamb's wife. Christ's appearance

> was that of a fresh, lovely youth, clad in grey cloth, very plain and neat, (at this time I had never heard of the Quakers or their habit,) of a sweet, affable, and courteous carriage. I saw him embrace several poor, old, simple people, whose appearance was very contemptible and mean, without wisdom or beauty. I seeing this, concluded within myself, that though he appeared young, his discretion and wisdom were very great . . . At last he beckoned to me to come near him, of which I was very glad. I

went tremblingly and lowly . . . The Lamb's wife [was] a beautiful young woman, slender, modest, and grave, in plain garments, becoming and graceful. Her image was fully answering his, as a brother and sister.[35]

Some dreams served to confirm the dreamer's call to ministry. David Ferris (1707–79) dreamed of a large building, unfinished and lacking a pillar. The master builder arrives and informs David Ferris that he is to be that pillar, to support the structure.[36] Samuel Bownas, just after spending nearly a year in prison in 1703, dreamed of meeting George Fox, whom he had never encountered in the flesh, and who desired him to catch three fish. Samuel Bownas then succeeded in taking in fine fish, despite meagre equipment of a 'switch stick for a rod', a 'piece of thread for a line', and a 'crooked pin for a hook'.[37] Like the biblical apostles, Samuel Bownas went on to fish for other people.

Related to dreams are waking visions. Two years before his death, John Woolman, as he lay near death suffering from a serious infection, had an extraordinary experience that confirmed his years of working in ministry in solidarity with the oppressed.

I was brought so near the gates of death that I forgot my name. Being then desirous to know who I was, I saw a mass of matter of a dull gloomy colour, between the south and the east, and was informed that this mass was human beings in as great misery as they could be and live, and that I was mixed in with them and henceforth might not consider myself as a distinct or separate being. In this state I remained several hours. I then heard a soft, melodious voice, more pure and harmonious than any voice I had heard with my ears before, and I believed it was the voice of an angel who spake to other angels. The words were, 'John Woolman is dead.' I soon remembered that I once was John Woolman, and being assured that I was alive in the body, I greatly wondered what that heavenly voice could mean. I believed beyond doubting that it was the voice of an holy angel, but as yet it was a mystery to me.

I was then carried in spirit to the mines, where poor oppressed people were digging rich treasures for those called Christians, and heard them blaspheme the name of Christ, at which I was grieved, for his name to me was precious. Then I was informed that these heathens were told that those who oppressed them were the followers of Christ, and they said amongst themselves: 'If Christ directed them to use us in this sort, then Christ is a cruel tyrant.'[38]

As he pondered the meaning of this vision, the words of Paul in Galatians of being crucified with Christ came to him, and he came to understand that 'that language John Woolman is dead meant no more than the death of my own will'.[39] The struggle to imitate Jesus' example, 'Not my will but yours be done', runs through the hundreds of extant Quaker journals.

Because journals gave great attention to chronicling the writer's journeys in the ministry, a description of the travelling ministry as a spiritual practice is in order.

The Travelling Ministry

Travelling ministry played an important role in the Society of Friends from the earliest days. The expression itself gives notice of two facts: there were Friends who had particular gifts in the ministry and who were recognized as such,[40] and that inter-visitation played a key role in Quaker religious culture.

While it has always been a part of Quaker belief that anyone may be called to work in the ministry, it has been a part of Quaker experience that some are called to a greater responsibility for this work. Robert Barclay put it this way in his *Apology for the True Christian Divinity* in 1676:

If [ministry] be understood of a liberty to speak or prophesy by the Spirit, I say that all may do that, when moved thereunto, . . . but we do believe and affirm that some are more particularly called to the work of the ministry, and therefore are fitted of the Lord for that purpose; whose work is more constantly and particularly to instruct, exhort, admonish, oversee, and watch over their brethren; and that . . . there is something more incumbent upon them in that respect than upon every common believer.[41]

Earliest Friends travelled to share the Quaker understanding of the gospel with the wider society. As persecution moved Friends to place a hedge between themselves and 'the world's people', travelling in the ministry continued, but ministers tended to travel mostly among other Quakers.[42] Because, compared to other traditions with a more developed and elaborate hierarchy, Quakerism was more congregational in its structure, travelling ministers helped to keep alive the ties among communities of Friends. Especially in smaller or more isolated meetings, travelling ministers wove the web of community, giving the visited meetings a sense of being a part of the wider family of Quakers. These ministers revitalized the spiritual life of the meetings that they visited. Travelling ministers were often effective speakers who moved their hearers and invited them into a deeper spiritual experience. Additionally these travellers ministered to others in the silence, attaining to a feeling sense of the condition of others, to the spiritual benefit of the other worshippers.

The travelling ministry was a boon to the recipients. Yet we can also consider the institution of the travelling ministry from the standpoint of the travellers themselves and see it as a kind of spiritual practice. The minister travelled only in response to a leading, to an interior call to undertake a particular journey. At times, a minister would feel led to travel and would sense that another minister might be similarly called. The first would ask the second to join her or him on the journey. The spiritual relationship between the two travellers would then be part of the experience.

To travel in the ministry was to step out of the ordinary

affairs of life. The community back home would help to care for family responsibilities, so that the minister could be free to travel. A journey might last several years, or the minister's life might end before returning home, as was the case with John Woolman, who died of smallpox in York, England, across the Atlantic from his home in Mt Holly, New Jersey. British Friend Elizabeth Hooten (d. 1672) met her death in distant Jamaica; Job Scott (1751–93) died in Ballitore, Ireland. A travelling minister's task was to be sensitive and faithful to leadings every step of the way, as she or he visited congregations and individuals and worshipped with them, whether that be in their regular meeting for worship, a special 'appointed' public meeting, or a private 'opportunity' with an individual or household. In a sense, to travel in the ministry was to be on a mobile retreat, or even a pilgrimage. Like a pilgrimage, travelling in the ministry offered opportunities for reflection, interior watchfulness. Travelling required a more direct reliance upon God because one was not in one's usual social setting and faced the physical discomforts and risks of travel that existed at that time. While travelling to visit Wyalusing, a settlement of Delaware nation, John Woolman offered these reflections on the experience of travelling in the ministry: 'I had this day often to consider myself as a sojourner in this world, and a belief in the all-sufficiency of God to support his people in their pilgrimage felt comfortable to me, and I was industriously employed to get to a state of perfect resignation.'[43]

Although not the same, this attitude is somewhat reminiscent of the practice of exile among early Celtic monastics, who would travel far from their homeland as an ascetical exercise.[44] Celtic exile or pilgrimage (*peregrinatio*) was a type of renunciation that also embraced the work of a missionary. Quaker ministers often travelled 'under the weight of a concern', such as a leading to work to bring slavery to an end, and were in that sense also missionaries.

Travelling in Company

Ministers seldom travelled alone. The common practice was to travel with at least one other person. Journeying in company developed bonds of deep friendship among ministers, and the relationship had deep spiritual value. In company there was the opportunity to engage in common discernment. One's motives could always be checked in conversation with the other, so that both could be more faithful to leadings. This practice of travelling together was also a kind of spiritual formation, as the more experienced minister would offer guidance to the younger.

Since the form of the journal itself stressed the public work in the ministry, journals often say regrettably little about the relationships forged between ministers who travelled together. The journals of Catherine Payton Phillips (1727–94) and Mary Peisley Neale (1717–57), however, offer some hints of the bonds of affection that sustained travelling ministers as they faced the challenges of travel in the eighteenth century.

Mary Peisley was the elder of the two and more experienced than Catherine Phillips, who was still young when they journeyed together.[45] Catherine Phillips repeatedly refers to Mary as her 'dear friend and companion'. 'We had been companions together in many probations, and our union in the Truth was strong.'[46] 'Our meeting was attended with divine consolation and our union in the Truth was renewed and enlarged.'[47] 'We met in wonted affection'.[48]

Catherine Phillips wrote to Mary about proposed travels in the ministry, rejoicing in their continued unity and 'sympathy of spirit'. She expressed her hopes in what borders on prayer: 'Oh! may we both be preserved near to the fountain of life, and then we must be near each other in the fellowship of the gospel, which distance of space cannot hinder, nor time efface; but it will centre with our spirits in that unchangeable state of felicity we humbly hope for.'[49] Mary's response expressed her love for Catherine Phillips and acknowledged a 'likeness of souls' between the two.

They sailed to America and travelled extensively throughout the north-east colonies of New England in 1754. In New York they felt led to separate for a time, even though they had been 'favoured with a great unity of spirit' to this time. Friends who travelled together often discerned that they were led for a time in different directions, so this was not so unusual.[50] From October to February they journeyed separately. Their reunion was 'attended with Divine consolation, under a sense of the protection of Providence having been over us in our absence from each other; and our union in the Truth was renewed and strengthened'.[51]

Mary Peisley described their relationship in touching terms:

> Through mercy our love for each other is not decreased by our separation, but much otherwise; and it is no wonder that we should be made more near and dear to each other, considering how much we have been led in the same track of suffering since separated, as well as together. This indeed must be the case with all them that know a growth in the Truth; their love in it for each other will increase, though the ties of natural affection may, by length of time and absence, in some degree be weakened.[52]

Friendship as a spiritual practice in western Christianity dates back at least as far as the early Cistercians in the twelfth century. Friendship blossomed among Quaker ministers, but the reticence of journalists invites imaginative reflection from readers as to the details of their spiritual friendship, especially in this day that seeks to recover the spirituality of friendship as a resource for the inner life.

Friendship in Times of Suffering

In times of persecution, Friends who travelled together offered tremendous support to one another, as did Katharine

Evans and Sarah Cheevers when they were prisoners of the Inquisition from 1658 to 1662. Although they were at times separated, for as long as a year's time, during their imprisonment, they offered one another solace and steadfastness as they were able despite the efforts of the officers of the Inquisition to break their spirits.[53]

Lest this reminder of the Inquisition be a painful thing to have brought to mind for Roman Catholic readers, let us also note the journey of the Quaker minister Stephen Grellet (1773–1855) to Rome in 1819, where he visited Pope Pius VII and visited the papal and inquisitorial prisons. The two spoke of reformations in the Inquisition, and the pope expressed his pleasure that Stephen Grellet had noted the changes: '[The pope] expressed his hope that the time was not far distant when Inquisitions everywhere will be totally done away. He assented to the sentiment that God alone has a right to control the conscience of man, and that the weapons of the Christian should not be carnal but spiritual.'[54]

A Modest Revival

In the early decades of the twentieth century, many unprogrammed meetings ceased the practice of recording ministers.[55] With the decline of the tradition of acknowledging those particularly called to the public ministry, the practice of the travelling ministry also diminished. What arose to take its place was the visiting speaker, a teaching ministry in which someone would offer a lecture or lead a workshop. Whatever its merits, it was not the same thing. First of all, the speaker prepared her or his presentation in advance. The Holy Spirit could inspire someone at any time, and certainly in advance of that person's arrival at the meeting that invited her or him. The presentation, however, would remain planned, not a direct response to the needs of a particular group, whom the speaker often would not even have met before. The speaker's words could be 'in the life', but would not arise out of the direct experience of the group. Second, the lecture or workshop would not usually occur in the direct context of group worship. Travelling ministers also nurtured their hosts in the silence of worship, and this kind of ministry would not occur in a lecture in the same way. In recent years among Friends there has been a revival of the travelling ministry, and though this movement is as yet a modest beginning, many are excited about its potential to renew Friends in this day.

Elders – 'A Whetstone'

In addition to ministers, who spoke regularly in meetings for worship and who travelled widely among Friends, there were elders. Elders stayed closer to home and found themselves moved to speak less frequently, but they offered spiritual nurture to the meeting. Robert Barclay used these words to describe elders:

> Also besides these who are thus particularly called to the ministry, and constant labour in the word and doctrine, there are also the elders, who though they be not moved to a frequent testimony by way of declaration in words, yet as such are grown up in the experience of the blessed work of truth in their hearts, they watch over and privately admonish . . . and look that . . . peace, love, unity, concord and soundness be preserved in the church of Christ.[56]

Quaker journals, influenced as they were by Puritan antecedents, focused on the public ministry. Recorded ministers, as Public Friends, were encouraged to write journals that were published after their death, but this expectation did not extend to the homebody elders. As a result, the history of eldering is not documented in anything like the detail for the ministers.

One exception is the Dublin physician John Rutty (1698–1775), who left behind a 'spiritual diary'. It is a series of notes and fragments rather than a sustained narrative or reflection. Nevertheless, in one entry this Irish Friend wrote of his office as elder in these words: 'Though not a minister, the Lord has made me a whetstone to the ministers, and blessed my station as such!'[57]

Elders and ministers met together to discuss the quality of vocal ministry and the general spiritual state of their meetings. Elders had the responsibility of guiding and encouraging young ministers. Like the elders of the ancient Christian monastic tradition, they were a font of spiritual advice and wisdom. Elders were the keepers of a tradition that was largely oral because the intuitive nature of Quaker experience made it so difficult to capture in words. A Friend in the Conservative tradition once described to me the eldering of a Friend steeped in the old ways: he could guide others into a deeper experience of worship the way that a divining rod points to water. Without a word spoken, those close to him simply felt themselves irresistibly drawn more fully into an awesome sense of God's presence. By word and by example, elders nurtured the inward life. Those led to this work have been called 'nursing fathers and mothers'.[58]

It is a difficult balancing act to be the conservators of tradition, especially when that tradition itself has a commitment to be open to the revelation of new truth. Elders did not always walk this knife's edge successfully. At times, as a body, elders became stodgy and stuffy, holding to the letter more than the Spirit who gives life. As a result, to be 'eldered' at times meant simply to be harshly criticized, to be upbraided for not adhering to the decorum of Quaker culture. At other times the elders' tendency for conservation clashed with the ministers' bent for innovation, and this played a sad role in the schisms of the nineteenth century.

Like the recording of ministers, the role of elders decreased sharply among most Friends through much of the twentieth century. In recent years, however, the elders' work of spiritual nurture to others and of centring the meeting in worship has undergone a modest but enthusiastic revival. As Friends have sought to steer a course between the two extremes of too much control, on the one hand, and confusion, on the other, there has emerged an appreciation of the modicum of order that can sustain life and offer it direction.

Advices and Queries

One more Quaker spiritual practice is the worshipful consideration of advices and queries.

> Dearly beloved Friends, these things we do not lay upon you as a rule or form to walk by, but that all, with the measure of light which is pure and holy, may be guided; and so in the light walking and abiding, these may be fulfilled in the Spirit, not from the letter, for the letter killeth, but the Spirit giveth life.[59]

These words form the conclusion of the earliest surviving collection of 'advices'. The weighty Friends gathered at Balby in 1656 issued an epistle intended to fortify Friends in their faith and to encourage them to live attentive to the 'Spirit that giveth life'.

Because they treat the same subjects, advices and queries have been combined among some Friends in recent years, but historically the difference has been that queries were formed in the interrogative mode and advices in the imperative. They have changed in their focus and application over time. At first they were eminently practical. The epistle from the Yorkshire town of Balby urged Friends to look after marrying and burying (since these were otherwise the affairs of a state Church to which Quakers did not adhere) and to caring for the needs of widows, orphans, and the poor. Queries began just as practically. In 1682 the first queries asked which Friends were suffering for their testimony to truth. The purpose was to learn who needed practical help: assistance in obtaining release from prison, if possible, and material support for the prisoner's dependants. As the earliest generation began to pass away, a new concern arose to preserve what until then existed only in oral memory: 'How did Truth come to you?' Eventually the queries came to focus on matters of discipline and reflected Friends' growing ethical concerns. Queries from Philadelphia Yearly Meeting in the mid-1700s admonished Friends to avoid gambling, dancing, 'drinking drams' to excess, importing or buying slaves, and 'tattling, tale bearing, and meddling'. The queries urged Friends to bring up their children in a godly way, to take care of the poor and educate their children, and not to launch into business beyond their means.[60] Monthly meetings considered these queries and submitted written responses to them. The queries were a collective spiritual practice.

That collective dimension endures in a somewhat different way, but in more recent times Friends have used advices and queries more personally. Advices and queries have evolved into an individual devotional practice. Not meant to be answered by a mere 'yes' or 'no', they are instead intended to serve as lenses through which Friends examine their lives. Advices and queries invite sustained reflection and are a staple of contemporary Quaker spirituality. Contemporary Friends often frame queries to focus their reflection on a given matter of concern and to invite God's guidance on these reflections.

Advices and queries are published in the *Faith and Practice* or *Book of Discipline* of each yearly meeting. (A yearly meeting is a regional body within Quakerism, akin to a diocese in Roman Catholicism or a district in North American Methodism. 'Yearly meeting' is also the name for the annual session within that region, when Friends gather annually for worship and to conduct church affairs.) What follows is a selection of advices and queries currently used in Britain Yearly Meeting.[61]

Take heed, dear Friends, to the promptings of love and truth in your hearts. Trust them as the leadings of God whose Light shows us our darkness and brings us to new life.

Bring the whole of your life under the ordering of the spirit of Christ. Are you open to the healing power of

God's love? Cherish that of God within you, so that this love may grow in you and guide you. Let your worship and your daily life enrich each other. Treasure your experience of God, however it comes to you. Remember that Christianity is not a notion but a way.

Do you try to set aside times of quiet for openness to the Holy Spirit? All of us need to find a way into silence which allows us to deepen our awareness of the divine and to find the inward source of our strength. Seek to know an inward stillness, even amid the activities of daily life. Do you encourage in yourself and in others a habit of dependence on God's guidance for each day? Hold yourself and others in the Light, knowing that all are cherished by God.

Live adventurously. When choices arise, do you take the way that offers the fullest opportunity for the use of your gifts in the service of God and the community? Let your life speak. When decisions have to be made, are you ready to join with others in seeking clearness, asking for God's guidance and offering counsel to one another?

We are called to live 'in the virtue of that life and power that takes away the occasion of all wars'. Do you faithfully maintain our testimony that war and the preparation for war are inconsistent with the spirit of Christ? Search out whatever in your own way of life may contain the seeds of war. Stand firm in our testimony, even when others commit or prepare to commit acts of violence, yet always remember that they too are children of God.

Are you alert to practices here and throughout the world which discriminate against people on the basis of who or what they are or because of their beliefs? Bear witness to the humanity of all people, including those who break society's conventions or its laws. Try to discern new growing points in social and economic life. Seek to understand the causes of injustice, social unrest and fear. Are you working to bring about a just and compassionate society which allows everyone to develop their capacities and fosters the desire to serve?

Try to live simply. A simple lifestyle freely chosen is a source of strength. Do not be persuaded into buying what you do not need or cannot afford. Do you keep yourself informed about the effects your style of living is having on the global economy and environment?

We do not own the world, and its riches are not ours to dispose of at will. Show a loving consideration for all creatures, and seek to maintain the beauty and variety of the world. Work to ensure that our increasing power over nature is used responsibly, with reverence for life. Rejoice in the splendour of God's continuing creation.

5. THE TESTIMONIES

Quaker spirituality is both inward and outward. Friends have always expected the Holy Spirit to transform individuals and then guide them into ways to transform society. The mystical stream in Quakerism has a profound ethical dimension. In worship together Friends have experienced not only wordless union with God but also practical leadings to engage in concrete actions.

Friends have always held dear the belief that the Light would bring them into unity. Their pattern of worship is contemplative yet corporate, blossoming into experiences of deep communion and community. Similarly, Quakers have expected the Light of Christ to lead them in the same direction and toward the same goals. Because revelation is continuing, new leadings will come, but because the Spirit is consistent, certain principles will prevail. Friends have called these principles 'testimonies' because they witness to the wider world of the power of God to transform individuals and human society.

Although the testimonies have retained a recognizable character, the expression of them has changed and developed over the centuries. Earlier Friends often spoke of the testimonies in terms of specific actions, such as not taking oaths or refusing to take off their hats in deference to those whom the wider culture would regard as their social superiors. Modern Friends tend to think of the testimonies in more categorical ways, as deriving from central underlying convictions, which they express in terms such as integrity, simplicity, equality, and peace.

The testimonies, like Christianity itself, are radically counter-cultural. They challenge the values of a society based on unbridled greed, distrust, violence, and oppression. In the early days, the testimonies were elements of the Lamb's War, that inner struggle of good and evil in each individual's heart. Early Friends, like their Puritan contemporaries, hoped to change human society. They believed that the remaking of society began with private morality, and that the remaking of personal morality began with an opening of the heart. The testimonies were intended to open the heart by challenging the conscience and conduct of others, often in an alarming way so as to get their attention and get them to reflect on their own behaviour.

Integrity

'Truth' loomed large in the vocabulary of early Friends. The Light had brought them into truth: truth about their own capacity for sin, truth about God's power to overcome evil, truth about God's availability to all without mediation of creed, hierarchy, or outward ritual. They therefore regarded truth-telling as essential, which took shape in several practices.

The first was the refusal to take oaths. Jesus after all had forbidden swearing (Matthew 5:33-7), as did the Epistle of James (5:12). Other radical Christians such as the Anabaptists also refused to swear. Early Quakers argued that oaths imply a double standard: if one must take an oath to insure that one is honest, the implication is that otherwise one is not obliged to tell the truth. Friends preferred to refuse to take oaths and instead to speak as honestly as though they were under oath at all times. In the words of William Penn, 'People swear to the end that they may speak truth; Christ would have men speak truth to the end they might not swear'.[1]

The price of this refusal could be great in the early days of Quakerism. Under English law at that time, refusal to take an oath of allegiance to the king was punishable by forfeiture of all one's property and an indefinite term of imprisonment.

Truth-telling also extended to the market place. Quaker merchants charged a single price for their goods, rather than asking an unreasonably high price as the first move in a contest of bargaining with their customers. Friends regarded such haggling as dishonest. Ironically, such honesty brought prosperity to numerous Quaker merchants. Many purchasers found the single-price policy attractive. Shopping was no longer a verbal battleground. They could send their children to make purchases and know that merchants would not take advantage of their innocence.

Honest, plain speech extended to the names of months and days of the week, a practice shared with some Puritans. Christians do not worship Janus or Thor, so honouring them in the calendar was not considered truthful. Sunday became First Day. March became Third Month.

Numbering the months or the days of the week has largely fallen out of practice among Friends since the late nineteenth century. Friends of today reflect on the meaning of integrity in our time. How do we enact integrity in this era, when government officials do not tell the truth to the populace that elected them, when researchers willingly falsify data to win grants and professional esteem, when owners of much of the media allow selfish political interests to determine what they report as news, and when advertisers offer an image of the good life that anyone with a bit of spiritual wisdom knows is not true?

Equality

In the exhilarating experimentation of the days of the English Revolution, Friends were not alone among the social radicals in their attention to equality. The Levellers argued for elimination of the class distinctions in English society. Early Baptist ministers were often 'mechanick preachers' who were not formally educated 'divines'. Quakers both agreed with their Baptist contemporaries and moved beyond their position.

George Fox's early revelations about equality focused first on ministry. 'The Lord opened unto me that being bred at Oxford

or Cambridge was not enough to fit and qualify men to be ministers of Christ'.[2] God could call anyone to preach in meeting
for worship, female or male, young or old, learned or
unschooled.

Particularly scandalous to many contemporaries of early
Friends was the idea that a woman might preach. George Fox
wrote how he 'met with a sort of people that held women have
no souls, (adding in a light manner), No more than a goose. But
I reproved them, and told them, that was not right; for Mary
said, "My soul doth magnify the Lord, and my spirit hath
rejoiced in God my Saviour."'[3]

George Fox's pivotal spiritual experience of restoration to
the purity of the Garden of Eden led naturally to the conviction that spiritually regenerated women and men were once
again equals, as they were before the Fall.[3] He found equality
between women and men demonstrated by Sarah and
Abraham, who practised a mutuality between them.[5] Moses,
when God revealed the law to him, did not tell women to stay
'at home to wash the dishes',[6] but encouraged them in public
work of the religious life, 'God having poured his Spirit upon
the house of Israel, both males and females'.

In 1666 Margaret Fell published her *Women's Speaking
Justified, Proved and Allowed of by the Scriptures*. Her argument begins with reference to Genesis 1:27, a verse of critical
importance to many feminists of a later age:

> And first, when God created man in his own image, in the
> image of God created he them, male and female; and God
> blessed them, and God said unto them, 'Be fruitful and
> multiply.' Here God joins them together in his own image,
> and makes no such distinctions and differences as men
> do . . . And God hath put no such difference between the
> male and female, as men would make.

Her tract goes on to discuss Eve and the serpent and the positive role of many women in the Gospels and the apostolic
Church. *Women's Speaking Justified* challenges the prohibition
of women preaching that opponents based on passages from

Paul. Margaret Fell's point is that Paul did not say that God could not speak through a woman. Paul, according to early Friends, objected to a woman speaking in her own will in worship. To Quakers, the same objection applied equally to men. The tract concludes:

> It is evident that God made no difference, but gave his good Spirit, as it pleased him, both to Man and Woman, as Deborah, Huldah, and Sarah . . . and Anna the Prophetess . . .
>
> And Philip the Evangelist . . . had four Daughters . . . that did prophesie . . . And so let this serve to stop that opposing Spirit that would limit the Power and Spirit of the Lord Jesus, whose Spirit is poured upon all flesh, both Sons and Daughters, now in his Resurrection.[8]

Early Quaker theologian Elizabeth Bathurst in 1683 published *The Sayings of Women*, which records the utterances of women in Scripture. Her thesis is buried in the middle of the treatise: 'Thus we find many renowned Women recorded in the Old Testament, who had received a Talent of Wisdom and Spiritual Understanding from the Lord; as good Stewards thereof they improved and employed the same to the Praise and Glory of God.'[9]

Women are not merely permitted to speak in worship but are also obliged to exercise the gifts of ministry that God has given them:

> As Male and Female are made one in Christ Jesus, so Women receive an Office in the Truth as well as Men, and they have a Stewardship, and must give an account of their Stewardship to their Lord, as well as the Men: Therefore they ought to be faithful to God, and valiant for his Truth upon the Earth.[10]

Levelling Down

The Quaker testimony of equality also has its roots in the leading to refuse hat honour to those accustomed to it in the exaggerated courtesies of seventeenth-century English society. In part a refusal to doff one's hat or to 'bow and scrape' to one's so-called social superior, hat honour was intended to challenge the pride of the other person, since early Quakers understood pride to be a major obstacle to opening oneself to the experience of the Light. This challenge to pride was apparently quite successful, to judge from the results as recorded by George Fox:

> Oh, the rage and scorn, the heat and fury that arose! Oh, the blow, punchings, beatings, and imprisonments that we underwent for not putting off our hats to men! . . . The bad language and evil usage we received on this account are hard to be expressed, beside the danger we were sometimes in of losing our lives for this matter.[11]

Similarly shocking was the early Quaker practice of addressing all individuals by the singular second-person pronoun 'thou' or 'thee' rather than the formal and plural form 'you'. Friends defended this practice based on their commitment to honesty and integrity: it is inappropriate and not true to address a single person as though he or she were more than one. Here the testimonies of equality and integrity coincide. Likewise they refused to call people by such titles as 'Your Grace', or 'Your Majesty'. According to Robert Barclay, the use of such titles forced people to lie because often those called 'Your Excellency' or 'Your Honour' had neither excellency nor honour in them.[12] Such 'foolish and superstitious formalities' were devised only to feed human pride 'in the vain pomp and glory of this world'.[13]

Although Friends as a whole did not subscribe to the programme of the Levellers, who argued for abolishing all class distinctions, their practices of equality tended to level down rather than to level up. They treated others as their social equals rather than treating the poor as if they were aristocracy. Their intent was to bring the prideful away from the temptation to vanity, rather than to increase the temptation for all. But if Friends levelled down in terms of titles and address, they levelled up in terms of social justice. George Fox admonished merchants to charge a fair price. He had a good grasp of the rudiments of English law, and he exhorted judges to enact justice for all.[14] Similarly he counselled tax collectors to 'take heed of oppressing the poor'.[15] While in Derby prison, he learned that 'there was a young woman that was to be put to death for robbing her master'.[16] He interceded and successfully halted the execution, 'though they had her upon the ladder with a cloth bound over her face' to hang her. Early Friends were prophetic in their self-understanding, and like the prophets they called for justice.

Because Quakers believed that the Light was available to each person, they were open to its presence in people from other races and cultures. Mary Fisher visited the Muslim Sultan of Turkey. George Fox wrote a letter to the emperor of China (though it is doubtful that it reached him). When William Penn founded his Holy Experiment in Pennsylvania, he extended the notion of spiritual equality to the political realm in his efforts to practise justice with Native Americans. In the eighteenth century, John Woolman embodied this spirit of equality when he wrote in his *Journal* of his motivation to visit a settlement of the Delaware nation in Wyalusing. In chapter three, we looked at this passage in the context of discerning leadings, yet it also attests to the Quaker conviction that all human beings have access to the Spirit of God.

> Love was the first motion, and then a concern arose to spend some time with the Indians, that I might feel and understand their life and the spirit they live in, if haply I might receive some instruction from them, or they be in any degree helped forward by my following the leadings of Truth amongst them.[17]

Concern for equality has led Friends to pursue justice in many causes over the last three hundred years. In the eighteenth century Friends such as Anthony Benezet laboured on behalf of the poor, political refugees, Native Americans, and the enslaved. In the nineteenth century Lucretia Mott devoted herself to abolition of slavery, religious freedom, prison reform, and women's rights. In the twentieth century Elizabeth Watson has worked for civil rights in the United States, has been a dedicated feminist and a courageous spokesperson for gay and lesbian rights. Australian Friend Helen Bayes has been led to reflect and act on equality with regard to the rights of children. She has laboured in the areas of juvenile justice, child soldiers, and child sexual exploitation.[18]

Simplicity

Simplicity has to do with trust and with focus. In the Sermon on the Mount, Jesus admonished his followers not to worry about clothing and food (Matthew 6:25-33). A simple life is based in confidence in God's faithful providence. In addition, a simple life enables one to keep God at the centre. Concern with too many external things distracts one from the spiritual life. In more recent times Friends have come to see simplicity as linked with the commitment to social justice and to responsible stewardship of God's good creation.

Quaker understanding of simplicity evolved throughout their history. Earliest Friends along with their Puritan contemporaries opposed luxury and waste. Other early Friends made explicit the connection between simple living and social justice, as William Penn wrote in 1693: 'The very trimming of the vain world would clothe all the naked one.'[19]

By the eighteenth century, as Quakerism developed into an austere sectarian ideal, simplicity became a code of plainness that applied to dress language, home furnishings, and even the height of gravestones (once these became common among Quakers – earliest Quaker burial grounds had no markers). Margaret Fell saw the earlier inclinations toward the drab Quaker costume that was to become the uniform of the eighteenth and nineteenth centuries. She lamented this direction as a degeneration that focused on the letter rather than the Spirit – the very thing against which earliest Friends rebelled.

> Poor Friends [are] mangled in their minds, ... Christ
> Jesus saith, that we must take no thought what we shall
> eat, or what we shall drink, or what we shall put on, but
> bids us consider the lilies how they grow, in more royalty
> than Solomon. But contrary to this, we must look at no
> colours, nor make anything that is changeable colours as
> the hills are, nor sell them, nor wear them: but we must be
> all in one dress and one colour: this is a silly poor Gospel.
> It is more fit for us, to be covered with God's Eternal
> Spirit, and clothed with his Eternal Light, which leads us
> and guides us into righteousness.[20]

Some fifty years later, during that same era when plainness
was the mark of God's peculiar people set apart from the wider
world, a number of Friends reflected on the deeper implica-
tions of a simple life. Some Quakers on both sides of the
Atlantic were settling into a comfortable life as prosperous
merchants, fulfilling precisely the prophetic words of Margaret
Fell. They dressed in plain clothing, but of the costliest material. They followed the outward letter of Quaker custom but
lacked the inward reality so essential to Quaker spirituality.[21]
A group of reformers arose to call Friends back to their ideals,
whose most articulate spokesperson was John Woolman.

As a young man John Woolman was apprenticed to a shop-
keeper. Others recognized his talent and made some tempting
business offers, but he chose intentionally to simplify his life.

> My mind through the power of Truth was in a good degree
> weaned from the desire of outward greatness, ... so that a
> way of life free from much entanglements appeared best for
> me, though the income was small. I had several offers of
> business that appeared profitable, but ... I saw that a
> humble man with the blessing of the Lord might live on a
> little, and that where the heart was set on greatness, suc-
> cess in business did not satisfy the craving, but that in com-
> mon with an increase of wealth the desire of wealth
> increased.[22]

So he took up the life of a tailor as a manageable kind of work, in order to be able to devote more time to the spiritual life and have the freedom to travel under religious concerns, especially to labour on behalf of the oppressed in his day. Additionally, a simple life kept him economically and spiritually closer to the condition of the oppressed, whether enslaved Africans, Native Americans, or impoverished colonists, so that he could understand their life with greater empathy.

Simplicity is good for the practitioner, but it affects the wider environment as well. John Woolman reflected frequently on the relationship between simplicity and justice. This led him to consider the nature of work in the context of what he called 'living in accordance with the design of creation'. He found a kind of divine ecology at work. If people would lay aside all unnecessary luxuries and the desire for wealth, power and prestige, and attend to 'the right use of things', there would be meaningful employment for all. Only moderate labour would be required. Labour itself is good, but too much of it is not. When desires are out of hand, people want too many things. To acquire them, they either must overwork themselves, which does not leave them the energy or the frame of mind to cultivate a spiritual life, or they make others overwork on their behalf. The latter leads to oppression and injustice.

As with justice, simplicity is intricately interwoven with peace. A simple life redeems us from the greed that is the root of war. John Woolman urged his readers to look deeply into their own lives to see what could foster the conditions for war: 'May we look upon our treasures and the furniture of our houses and the garments in which we array ourselves and try whether the seeds of war have any nourishment in these our possessions or not.'[23]

Simplicity can inspire us to remake human society:

> Our gracious Creator cares and provides for all his creatures. His tender mercies are over all his works; and so far as his love influences our minds, so far we become interested in his workmanship and feel a desire to take

hold of every opportunity to lessen the distresses of the afflicted and increase the happiness of the creation. Here we have a prospect of one common interest from which our own is inseparable – that to turn all the treasures we possess into the channel of universal love becomes the business of our lives.[24]

Simplicity in our day has both inward and outward dimensions. Simplicity may no longer seem simple in an era of complex economics, international trade and labour practices, and awareness of our role in the web of ecology. The testimony itself is as important as ever, as is the need for openness to new leadings in how to respond to current injustice and environmental crises. Inwardly, simplicity remains essential in contemporary culture, which awards prestige on the basis of how busy and overworked one's life is, and where we are endlessly bombarded with information. Simplicity invites us to discernment, to pray for guidance to identify which of the many good causes in the world are our vocation, and to make choices that foster the interior spaciousness that allows us to attend to the Spirit of God.

Peace

The peace testimony is likely the most widely known of Quaker ethical commitments. Like the other testimonies, it has evolved over time and has taken a variety of expressions.

Early Leadings

Like other testimonies, the peace testimony began as an individual leading. George Fox had been committed to prison under a charge of blasphemy. As George Fox explained, he was jailed for witnessing to the possibility of a sinless life, abiding in 'Christ my Saviour [who] hath taken away my sin'.[25] To live in this sinless state is to be inwardly restored to Paradise, the state of innocence before sin entered the world, bringing alienation and division in its wake. The peace testimony witnesses to the power of God to overcome alienation and achieve reconciliation. In prison the jailers recognized George Fox's capacity as a leader: he was ruthlessly honest, concerned for justice, and endowed with a spiritual power that could only come from a life centred in God. At that time in England, many Puritans were zealous to establish a godly commonwealth, and they believed that this could happen only if earnest Christians fought in battle to maintain power in government for the Puritan party. Soldiers and army commissioners came to George Fox and offered him release from prison if he would accept a captaincy in Cromwell's army. George Fox recorded:

> But I told them that I lived in the virtue of that life and power that took away the occasion of all wars, and I knew from whence all wars did rise, from the lust according to James's doctrine . . . I told them that I was come into the covenant of peace which was before wars and strives were.[26]

He proclaimed that he lived in the power of God that overcame the roots of war. His statement that wars 'rise from the lust' echoes the Epistle of James. Our post-Freudian era has limited the range of the word 'lust', but in George Fox's day the word could refer to any uncontrolled desire. The Epistle contrasts war with the peace that is rooted in divine wisdom.[27] The values of an unredeemed world differ from those of a life transformed by the Prince of Peace. Wars arise from inner desires — that is where the conflict begins. Because God resolved that conflict in the heart of George Fox through the victory of the Lamb, George Fox could not participate in outward wars. War was obsolete; his life was centred in love.

Other early Quakers came to pacifism through personal experience of war. William Dewsbury described how he came to the conviction that war is inconsistent with the teachings of Jesus. As in other wars waged by Christians, preachers of war invoked Judges 5:23 to condemn any who might resist the call to violence. William Dewsbury's experience was that the real conflict between good and evil lay in the human heart, and so outward weapons should be put away.

> At that time did the wars begin in this nation, and the men called ministers cried, 'Curse ye Meroz, because they went not forth to help the Lord against the mighty.' Then I was willing to give my body to death, in obedience to my God, to free my soul from sin, and I joined with that little remnant which said they fought for the gospel, but I found no rest to my soul amongst them. And the word of the Lord came unto me and said, 'Put up thy sword into thy scabbard; if my kingdom were of this world, then would my children fight', which word enlightened my heart and discovered the mystery of iniquity, and that the Kingdom of Christ was within, and the enemies [were] within, and [were] spiritual, and my weapons against them must be spiritual, the power of God. Then I could no longer fight with a carnal weapon against a carnal man.[28]

James Nayler likewise proposed that the inward struggle between good and evil is the genuine battleground. Outward strife and war are only a distraction and a temptation to ignore the unfinished inward conflict.[29] People project their inner turmoil onto the outer world, and this is the root of violence. He further proposed that the persecution that Quakers experienced from others was also a violent projection of interior conflict.

The year 1659 brought a political crisis. The Puritan commonwealth was at stake. The gentry, who commanded their own military forces, wanted to restore the monarchy. Quakers along with other religious radicals had dedicated their lives to building a society with freedom and justice, and now all that was at risk. Puritan leaders called on the radicals to enrol in the militia as commissioners. It was a tempting – and desperate – situation, and some did join, including a small number of Quakers. For the first time, even the Quakers were invited to share in the power. George Fox was agonized, confused, and depressed for weeks as he struggled with this dilemma. But clearness came, and he concluded that not even saving the dream of a transformed society could justify violence, since the violence itself would demonstrate that the transformation had not been real. The monarch returned, a Cavalier Parliament bent on revenge prevailed, and those who dissented from the state Church faced periodic and at times intense persecution for nearly forty years, until the Act of Toleration was passed in 1689.

A Corporate Testimony

What began as individual leadings became a corporate testimony. Margaret Fell wrote to Charles II and Parliament in 1660, describing the Friends' testimony 'against all strife and wars'. Again we hear the echoes of the Epistle of James:

> We are a people that follow after those things that make for peace, love and unity; it is our desire that others' feet may walk in the same, and do deny and bear our testimony against all strife, and wars, and contentions that come from the lusts that war in the members, that war in the soul, which we wait for, and watch for in all people, and love and desire the good of all.[30]

In response to persecution, and to the dawning realization that the whole of England was not going to become Quaker, Friends tended to withdraw from larger society into a separate existence as God's peaceable people. In the American colonies, however, William Penn worked to establish a haven of religious freedom among colonists and friendship with the Delaware nation without either a militia or forts. This Holy Experiment lasted three quarters of a century, until Friends chose to resign from the legislature rather than violate their peace testimony when the English crown insisted on a militia during the Seven Years' War with the French. William Penn's peaceful vision was wider than the borders of the colony that bore his father's name. His *Essay toward the Present and Future Peace of Europe* proposed a European council similar to the United

Nations in some ways. Unlike the current European Union, his design included Russia and Turkey. William Penn's notion of peace had room for a variety of cultures.

Like their predecessor, the Quaker reformers of the mid-eighteenth century saw that greed led the way to injustice and oppression and ultimately bred conditions for war. Justice and peace were inextricably interwoven. John Churchman and others also refused on grounds of conscience to pay taxes levied to support the Seven Years' War, preferring instead to 'suffer distraint of goods'. War tax resistance is a venerable as well as a contemporary Quaker practice that has continued to this day among a minority of Friends.

Engaging the Wider World

The sectarian 'hedge' around Friends slowly lowered in the nineteenth century, as they made common cause with promoters of abolition, women's rights, temperance, and other social reforms. The peace testimony continued to evolve and now included efforts for international reconciliation. English Friend Joseph Sturge, with the blessing of London Yearly Meeting, followed a leading in 1854 to travel to the court of Tsar Nicholas I to seek to prevent the Crimean War, a conflict in the 1850s for the control of south-eastern Europe, in which England allied with Turkey and France against Russia. The Russian emperor received him favourably, but the British government proceeded with war. Joseph Sturge faced severe criticism from his fellow citizens upon his return, many of whom were swept up in war fever and denounced his peace mission as treasonous. Undefeated by this humiliation, after the war he promoted a relief programme in the Baltic. Similarly in 1871 British Friends provided relief following the devastations of the Franco-Prussian War. British and American Friends shared the Nobel Peace Prize in 1947 for their massive efforts to relieve suffering in Europe after the two world wars.

The peace testimony developed in other new directions in the twentieth century. Working with others, Friends helped to initiate Civilian Public Service camps for conscientious objectors during the Second World War. After the war, Friends in Europe brought together young diplomats from East and West to meet and build bonds of respect and friendship that could counter the propaganda of the Cold War. The Friends Committee on National Legislation lobbied for issues of peace and disarmament on Capitol Hill in Washington, D.C. The era of the Vietnam War brought new methods of public protest and a vision for a new society grounded in peace and justice.

'One Small Plot of Heaven'

What might be the future expression of Quaker testimonies? Elise Boulding, a Quaker sociologist and peace researcher who has described herself as a student of the future, offers insights. She has pointed to the family as the centre of a spiritual practice. She defines family very widely, to include not only what comes to mind when most people hear the word, but also a household in which a person lives alone. The word for her also embraces the family in which the couple's love for each other is not recognized by state because both are male or female. In other words, the family is for everyone. The family is, she suggests, a laboratory for a culture of peace and justice. It is where the Quaker testimonies can be learned and exercised. It is a 'practice ground in making history' and a 'way into the future'.[31] The family has an eschatological dimension; it is 'one small plot of heaven'. From the family of our own household we can branch out to embrace the wider human family and the family of all life.

The home has been at the heart of Quaker spirituality. Rufus Jones described the spiritual life in the family of his boyhood:

> When I was too young to have any religion of my own, I had come to a home where religion kept its fires always burning. We had very few 'things', but we were rich in invisible wealth. I was not 'christened' in a church, but I was sprinkled from morning till night with the dew of reli-

gion. We never ate a meal which did not begin with a hush of thanksgiving: we never began a day without 'a family gathering' at which mother read a chapter of the Bible, after which there would follow a weighty silence. These silences, during which all the children of our family were hushed with a kind of awe, were very important features of my spiritual development. There was work inside and outside the house waiting to be done, and yet we sat there hushed and quiet, doing nothing. I very quickly discovered that something real was taking place. We were feeling our way down to that place from which living words come and very often they did come. Someone would bow and talk with God so simply and quietly that he never seemed far away. The words helped to explain the silence. We were now finding what we had been searching for. When I first began to think of God I did not think of him as very far off . . . he seemed to be there with us in the living silence. My first steps in religion were thus acted. It was a religion which we did together. Almost nothing was said in the way of instructing me. We all joined together to listen for God and then one of us talked to him for the other. In these simple ways my religious disposition was being unconsciously formed and the roots of my faith in unseen realities were reaching down far below my crude and childish surface thinking.[32]

The decorum of Quaker culture made most Friends of earlier times more reticent than Rufus Jones to discuss spirituality in family life. In our day many people are struggling to find the right balance between their families and their work that places such demands on them. It may be time for more Friends to articulate a spirituality of family as a laboratory for the testimonies.

Marriage and parenthood have been my best spiritual teachers, and often the most demanding while at the same time the most forgiving. Caring for young children complicated my life beyond imagination but also taught me the most about simplicity because it invited me to see what was truly most important in my life. Family life has also offered me lessons in integrity as it brought me face to face with my own shortcomings and limitations. If, as the old maxim goes, 'charity begins at home', so does peace, because the love that blossoms into peace is learned from those closest to us. Equality also came to the fore, as two professionals sought to share domestic duties equitably. For me, the family has been a training ground for the testimonies. Not all families will have children, but I believe that all of them will pose opportunities for practising the core values of the Quaker tradition. If the testimonies are an eschatological witness, then the family as their practice ground can very well be 'one small plot of heaven'.

6. THE FACING BENCH

In many meetinghouses, the persons with responsibility for discerning when worship is coming to a close sit on a bench facing the rest of the congregation. Historically, the facing bench (sometimes a raised platform, the 'ministers' gallery') was where the ministers and elders of the community sat in worship. Since ministers were the ones who most often spoke during meeting for worship, the purpose of the facing bench was so that their words could be more readily heard. I have gathered in this chapter some Friends from across the centuries, to include more voices and to offer some beloved passages that have inspired Friends over the years.

The Immediate Presence of God: Dorothy White and Rufus Jones

Dorothy White (c. 1630–85) was second only to Margaret Fell as a writer of early Quaker tracts, but little of her life is known. These words from her *A Trumpet Sounded out of the Holy City, Proclaiming Deliverance to the Captives*, written in 1662, resound with hope and triumph, even though persecution against dissenters raged at that time. Her words are an intense celebration of God's presence as they internalize the eschatological language of numerous biblical passages.[1]

And now is the glory of all nations come, and the bridegroom's voice is heard in the land of the redeemed, who are come out again of Egypt, who are become the first fruits unto God, and to the Lamb. These shall arise in the glorious power. These shall mount upward, as upon eagle's wings . . . These shall come unto the holy mountain, where the feast of fat things is prepared . . . Mount Zion, where the Song of Moses and the Lamb is sounded before his throne, who hath now appeared in his eternal glory . . . And so blessed are all whose feet are upon the rock, the foundation of God which standeth sure. I will make my people as Mount Zion, saith the Lord of holiness, and as the walls are about Jerusalem, even so is the Lord God round about his people. And blessed are they that dwell . . . under the over-shadowing of the Almighty . . . And now rejoice, thou barren womb, which hath brought forth the first begotten of God, for more shall be thy children than of her that was the married wife. For the vine shall yield its increase, and the blessing of the Lord shall multiply upon the works of his hands, his new creation. And the former heavens are passing away, and the new heavens are created again, wherein the Son of Righteousness shineth in his beauty, where the glory of the Lord filleth the earth.[2]

Rufus Jones, the most widely known Friend during the twentieth century, both studied and lived the mystical life. Philosopher, historian, orator, ecumenist, and social activist, he wrote more than fifty books, and his words have made spirituality come to life for generations of readers.

The history of religion through the ages reveals the fact that there have been multitudinous ways of worshiping God, all of them yielding real returns of life and joy and power to large groups of men. At its best and truest, however, worship seems to me to be *direct, vital, joyous, personal experience and practice of the presence of God.*

The very fact that such a mighty experience as this is possible means that there is some inner meeting place between the soul and God; in other words, that the divine and human . . . are not wholly sundered . . . [God] is a Being who can pour His life and energy into human souls, even as the sun can flood the world with light and resident forces, or as the sea can send its refreshing tides into all the bays and inlets of the coast, or as the atmosphere can pour its life-giving supplies into the fountains of the blood in the meeting place of the lungs; or, better still, as the mother fuses her spirit into the spirit of her responsive child . . .

It must be held, I think, as Emerson so well puts it, that there is 'no bar or wall in the soul' separating God and men. We lie open on one side of our nature to God, who is the Oversoul of our souls, the Overmind of our minds, the Overperson of our personal selves. There are deeps in our consciousness which no private plumb line of our own can sound; there are heights in our moral conscience which no ladder of our human intelligence can scale; there are spiritual hungers, longings, yearnings, passions, which find no explanation in terms of our physical inheritance or of our outside world. We touch upon the coasts of a deeper universe, not yet explored or mapped, but no less real and certain than this one in which our mortal senses are at home. We cannot explain our normal selves or account for the best things we know – or even for our condemnation of our poorer, lower self – without an appeal to and acknowledgment of a divine Guest and Companion who is the real presence of our central being.[3]

The Experience of Worship: Isaac Penington and Howard Brinton

Isaac Penington (1616–79), the son of the Lord Mayor of London, enjoyed more education than most early Quakers. He was a mystical seeker before he came to Friends in the years 1656–8. His words offer a thoughtful description of the corporate dimension of Quaker worship.

And this is the manner of their worship. They are to wait upon the Lord, to meet in the silence of flesh, and to watch for the stirrings of his life, and the breakings forth of his power amongst them. And in the breakings forth of that power they may pray, speak, exhort, rebuke, sing, or mourn, &c. according as the Spirit teaches, requires, and gives utterance. But if the Spirit do not require to speak, and give to utter, then every one is to sit still in his place (in his heavenly place I mean), feeling his own measure, feeding thereupon, receiving therefrom, into his spirit, what the Lord giveth. Now, in this is edifying, pure edifying, precious edifying; his soul who thus waits, is hereby particularly edified by the Spirit of the Lord at every meeting. And then also there is the life of the whole felt in every vessel that is turned to its measure: insomuch as the warmth of life in each vessel doth not only warm the particular, but they are like a heap of fresh and living coals, warming one another, insomuch as a great strength, freshness, and vigour of life flows into all. And if any be burthened, tempted, buffeted by Satan, bowed down, overborne, languishing, afflicted, distressed, &c., the estate of such is felt in Spirit, and secret cries, or open (as the Lord pleaseth), ascend up to the Lord for them, and they many times find ease and relief, in a few words spoken, or without words, if it be the season of their help and relief with the Lord.[4]

Howard Brinton (1884–1973) taught physics in several colleges in the United States before directing Pendle Hill, a Quaker study centre near Philadelphia, for many years. His contemporaries included Rufus Jones, Douglas Steere, and Thomas Kelly – a golden era of spiritual writers among Friends in the liberal and mystical tradition. In the following passage on Quaker worship, he hesitantly struggles to describe an inward experience that lies at the edge of human language – and even human consciousness. Like the apostle Paul's words in 2 Corinthians 12 – 'I know a person in Christ who fourteen years ago was caught up to the third heaven' – I suspect that Howard Brinton's words are autobiographical yet humbly stated in the third person.

> The worshipper sits down in silence. He seeks to compose his wandering thoughts. How shall he begin in order that his worship may not become a dreamy reverie? Perhaps by repeating a prayer, or verse of Scripture or poetry. As he progresses, he may be able to offer a prayer of his own which emerges with thoughts which have to do with the routine problems of his daily life. He must not fear to express selfish desires, for, above all, he must be sincere. He may then find that these desires, when expressed before God, assume a different form, proportion and direction. After a time something may come before his mind, a past event, the future possibility, a saying or occurrence in the Bible or elsewhere on which his attention becomes fixed. This focus of attention is now seen, not in a secular, but in a religious context it is viewed in its eternal rather than its temporal aspect.

> The will and feelings of the worshipper become stirred as the thought before him glows with life and power. He no longer feels that he himself is searching, but that he is being searched through. There is a growing sense of divine presence. Truth is not thought about, but perceived and enjoyed. It may be the point is reached at which the worshipper finds he must communicate to the meeting what has come to him. Or he may resolve to act at some time in the future in accordance with the Light which he has received. If he waits quietly and expectantly with the windows of his soul open to whatever Light may shine, he may lose all sense of separate existence and find himself aware only of the greater life on which his own is based. The sense of union with God may come unexpectedly. This occurs more often than is generally supposed, for it is frequently not recognized for what it is. Such complete self-forgetfulness cannot easily be reproduced in memory. There is the lower self-forgetfulness of sleep which cannot be remembered at

all, and there is, at the opposite pole, the higher self-forgetfulness in which every faculty of the soul is intensely awake, with the result that consciousness is widened to include what is beyond thought and memory.[5]

The Universal Light of Christ: Marjorie Sykes and Ham Sok Hon

Marjorie Sykes (1905–95), born in Yorkshire, graduated from Cambridge University, and went to India to teach in the city of Madras (now Chennai). During her sixty years in India she served as a school teacher and principal, a peace educator, a co-worker and translator of Rabindranath Tagore, and a teacher in Gandhi's ashram Sevagram, where she worked closely with Vinoba Bhave. Marjorie Sykes worked among Friends in Madras in the south, in Bengal, and in central India, and was fluent in Tamil, Bengali, and Hindi. Her Quakerism was rooted in a solidly Christian self-understanding, yet she acknowledged truth as she encountered it in other faiths, especially those she met in India. She could footnote Quaker truths with references to the Upanishads.

The living core of a religion is not to be sought in its outward observances, ceremonial, liturgy or festival (though it may be sought through them), nor yet in any intellectual world view which may emerge from its sacred writings; it is to be sought in the way it leads men, in the secret places of the heart, into the Presence of God . . . All living religion begins with this awed recognition of a Mystery and Power which is great beyond all comprehension, and yet is 'nearer than breathing and closer than hands and feet'. All living religion goes from this to a two-fold task: the human being is impelled to purify himself, to cleanse heart and mind and will, so that he may enter more and more fully into communion with that Reality and so fulfil the true purpose of his own life; at the same time he is impelled to share with other men his experience of the Mystery, and in so doing to use the words and symbols of his own age and country. Quakers also have a heritage of form and symbol, which was created to express a living truth of our experience; our very forms and symbols are a witness to the faith that God is beyond all forms and that the Free Spirit cannot be confined within any of its temporal symbols:

> 'The One Breath enters the world, taking a
>   myriad of forms,
> Even so the One,
> The innermost indwelling Life of all that is,
> Taketh a myriad of form –
> Yet is that One beyond all forms.'

> *(Katha-Upanishad)*

. . . The central purpose of all religion, of all worship, is salvation; it is to make men whole and *free* by turning them away from the self-centeredness of the 'natural man' and enabling them to find their True Centre . . . We all know the fruits of the Spirit, and recognize the beauty of holiness, in our own ancestral tree . . . The flowers of unselfish living may be found growing in other men's gardens and rich fruits of the Spirit may be tasted from other men's trees. They spring from the same Holy Spirit of Truth, the same seed of God, whose power moves us through Christ. . . . We do not desire that all should take the name of Quaker or the outward name of Christ. We do desire that all should be guided by 'that Spirit which is pure and holy', and that God will speak to them in whatever language, and through whatever symbol, can best bring them to the True Centre of their lives.[6]

Ham Sok Hon (1902–89), called by many 'the Gandhi of Korea', spent his lifetime promoting non-violence and democratic rights. His life mirrored the sad history of Korea in the twentieth century: he suffered imprisonment by the occupying

Japanese and Russian forces, then crossed the Thirty-Eighth Parallel into South Korea, where he was a political prisoner of oppressive Korean regimes. He came to call prison his 'university of life', not only because it was a place of serious self-study but also because it taught him lessons in political life that he could never learn in ordinary university. Twice nominated for the Nobel Peace prize, this gentle prophet inspired many in his homeland and beyond.

Ham Sok Hon came to Quakerism through the Christianity he had encountered as a younger man, first Presbyterianism, then the Non-Church Movement. In Quakerism he found a means that enabled him to blend his Christianity with his Asian identity. Quaker pacifism offered him a Christian vehicle for the non-violence in Taoism that had moved him deeply when he studied Taoist texts during a prison term. The Quaker belief that the Light of Christ was available to all people everywhere gave him a way to affirm the gifts of Asian thought.

> I don't want my salvation, if it is only for myself. The salvation should be for everyone in the whole world. Even the communists, atheists, heretics, evangelists, and shamanists, all of them should have the salvation, that is the real salvation.[7]

> I love both Lao-tzu and Chuang-tzu, but it is Jesus Christ that I believe in. There is no God for me except His God.[8]

> The Church labelled me a heretic . . . Their reasons were chiefly, "He has forsaken the Cross", or "He doesn't pray", or "He is too Oriental." But I do not deny the Cross. I only say that the Cross is not for us simply to adore and behold from a distance, rather we must strive to bear the Cross in our bodies. I do not neglect prayer. I only maintain that public prayer is all too often no more than formality and the self-flattery of men and thus we should avoid public prayer insofar as possible. Finally, I am prepared to fight with conviction against the rejection of things Oriental by

the Church. This is because most of the opposition to Confucianism and Buddhism is done only on the basis of narrow denominationalism without any understanding of their real meaning.[9]

Our thoughts should not be too narrow . . . The laws of the universe and of life are poly-dimensional. It should not make a difference if we have different thoughts. No two people have the same face. Such is life. Why do people insist that my religion and my thoughts should be the same as theirs? . . .Varieties of life and thought should grow.[10]

If anyone said, 'My painting, my poem, and my song are the only great ones', and declares 'Others' paintings, poems and songs are terrible!', he does not understand the real meaning of the arts.[11]

It is like opening a mountain path by the cutting of a tunnel from either side of the mountain. This tunnelling of the mountain begins in totally opposite directions, yet ultimately, the aim is the same. By approaching the centre [essence] of the mountain [Truth] from different directions, they will meet at the mid-point of the mountain.[12]

The Wilderness and the Dark Night: Samuel Bownas and Sandra Cronk

Samuel Bownas (1676–1753), a minister writing about 1750, used the image of the biblical wilderness to describe the experience of inward purification and the transition from bondage to the freedom of grace. For him, the wandering in the desert symbolized the interior aridity of this purgation: familiar spiritual practices no longer sufficed. Only a radical attentiveness to and reliance on 'our spiritual Moses' could bring the faithful to the inward Promised Land. Samuel Bownas' language is in some ways reminiscent of the Carmelite mystics John of the Cross and Teresa of Ávila.

> We must be brought out of the bondage of corruption under spiritual Pharaoh and Egypt, into the wilderness, before we can offer acceptably unto God.
>
> This state is figuratively called a wilderness, a way we have not trod in, showing thereby the necessity of depending on our guide, our spiritual Moses, that must go before and take care of our support. For in this wilderness state we have no good, no water, no right refreshment but what this our leader provides and administers to us. In this state we can neither pray nor do any religious act without the direction of our leader, so that we find the case is much altered with us to what it was in time past. For then we could pray, sing, preach, and perform other religious duties in our time, feeding and satisfying ourselves therewith, but now we are brought into the wilderness, where there is neither ploughing nor sowing. We can't now help ourselves by our own contrivance, and workings in our own wills, but here we must live a life of faith, wholly depending on him that will (if we faint not in our minds) bring us through to the heavenly Canaan. Thus we shall come in the Lord's time to experience the substance of those types and figures, under that legal dispensation to be substantially and spiritually fulfilled in our own minds by the operation of the Spirit of our Lord Jesus Christ, the substance and foundation of all true religion and ministry that is really profitable to the hearers.[13]

Sandra Cronk (1942–2000), a spiritual heir to Samuel Bownas, was a significant voice in the current renaissance of Quaker spirituality. Educated as a historian of religions, she ultimately found her vocation in offering spiritual nurture and training others in the ministries of contemplative prayer and spiritual nurture. Modern liberal Quakerism can tend toward too optimistic a view of the self, settling for a kind of joy that can in the long run prove superficial and incapable of answering the deeper questions of life. Sandra Cronk offered a corrective to this risk, holding up the rigorous self-honesty of earlier Friends, and inviting us to the joy of resurrection that could come only after the inward cross. Drawing consciously on John of the Cross, whose insights she brought into conversation with traditional Quaker spirituality, she wrote on the 'dark night journey', which she aptly described as 'inward repatterning toward a life centred in God'. This deeper encounter with God requires the stripping away of 'two pillars' of 'misplaced faith', two 'false sources of security': 'self' and 'god'.

> As the old self cracks open we discover not the annihilation we had feared but a deeper 'I'. This deeper 'I' is not a possession that can be remade through all our efforts at self-improvement. This deepest self is a gift from God. Recognizing that we exist because of God's gift of ourselves makes a new structure possible in our lives . . . Our love for others springs from the awareness that others are also gifts from God. Our love does not come from our efforts to make ourselves more loving and caring by dint of our own ego-centered struggles. The journey which may have looked at first as though it were distancing us from other people and from the needs of this world has brought us to an inward place where we can love others with new depth because we are no longer the center of our own loving. Miraculously, with the movement to a deeper center in our lives, we are able to release our hold on God as a possession . . . We had wanted the fruits of a close relationship with God, but we did not necessarily want God . . . In truth, we wanted to provide our own salvation. We wanted a god who would be yet another finite pillar under our control, a god that would take away the terror of facing that empty place which lurked at the limit of all finite things, and at the end of our 'self' . . . We recognize that it is not that our lives need to be opened to God. This imagery retains us in control; 'we' allow God to enter 'our' domain. Now we recognize that God invites us into the divine

life . . . This transformation marks our participation in Christ's crucifixion. In the darkness all reliance on our human efforts to bring salvation is shattered. The old self dies. Into emptiness God brings new life. 'I have been crucified with Christ; it is no longer I who live, but Christ who lives in me' (Gal. 2:20a). Our life becomes transparent to the eternal Word, Christ.[14]

The Spiritual Basis of Peace: The 1660 Declaration and William Rotch

In a declaration to the king in 1660, a group of Friends articulated their peace testimony. Because the Spirit of Christ is consistent, they could assure the king that Friends would not join any conspiracy to overthrow the monarchy with violence, as the apocalyptic group known as the Fifth Monarchy Men had attempted earlier that year.

> Our principle is, and our practices have always been, to seek peace, and ensue it, and to follow after righteousness and the knowledge of God, seeking the good and welfare and doing that which tends to the peace of all. We know that wars and fightings proceed from the lusts of men (as James 4:1-3), out of which lusts the Lord hath redeemed us, and so out of the occasion of war . . . All bloody principles and practices we . . . do utterly deny, with all outward wars, and strife, and fightings with outward weapons, for any end, or under any pretence whatsoever, and this is our testimony to the whole world . . . The spirit of Christ by which we are guided is not changeable, so as once to command us from a thing as evil, and again to move unto it; and we do certainly know, and so testify to the world, that the spirit of Christ which leads us into all Truth will never move us to fight and war against any man with outward weapons, neither for the kingdom of Christ, nor for the kingdoms of this world . . . Because the kingdom of Christ God will exalt, according to his promise,

and cause it to grow and flourish in righteousness. 'Not by might, nor by power [of outward sword], but by my spirit, saith the Lord.' (Zech. 4:6.) So those that use any weapon to fight for Christ, or for the establishing of his kingdom or government, both the spirit, principle, and practice in that we deny . . . And as for the kingdoms of this world, we cannot covet them, much less can we fight for them, but we do earnestly desire and wait, that by the word of God's power and its effectual operation in the hearts of men the kingdoms of this world may become the kingdoms of the Lord and of his Christ, that he might rule and reign in men by his spirit and truth, that thereby all people, out of all different judgements and professions might be brought into love and unity with God and one with another, and that they might all come to witness the prophet's words, who said, 'Nation shall not lift up sword against nation, neither shall they learn war any more.' (Isaiah 2:4; Micah 4:3.)[15]

Pacifism is often misunderstood as 'passivism', but the roots of the word mean 'to make peace'. Pacifism is action in obedience to God's will. We are reminded of this in the story of William Rotch (1734–1828), a Friend from Nantucket, where the Quaker community suffered much from both Patriots and British for its neutrality during the American Revolution. William Rotch had received some guns as payment of a debt some twelve years before. He had sold the muskets as hunting pieces, having first removed the bayonets, which he stored in a warehouse. The American forces demanded that he hand over the bayonets in 1776.

The time was now come to endeavour to support our testimony against war, or abandon it, as this very instrument was a severe test. I could not hesitate which to choose, and therefore denied the applicant. My reason for not furnishing them was demanded, to which I readily answered, 'As this instrument is purposely made and used for the destruction of mankind, I can put no weapon into a man's hand to destroy another, that I cannot use myself in the same way.' The person left me much dissatisfied. Others came, and received the same denial. It made a great noise in the country, and my life was threatened. I would gladly have beaten them into 'pruning hooks', but I took an early opportunity of throwing them into the sea.

A short time after I was called before a committee appointed by the court then held at Watertown near Boston, and questioned amongst other things respecting my bayonets.

I gave a full account of my proceedings, and closed it with saying, 'I sunk them in the bottom of the sea, I did it from principle. I have ever been glad that I had done it, and if I am wrong I am to be pitied.' The chairman of the committee Major Hawley (a worthy character) then addressed the committee and said, 'I believe Mr. Rotch has given us a candid account, and every man has a right to act consistently with his religious principles, but I am sorry that we could not have the bayonets, for we want them very much.'

The Major was desirous of knowing more of our principles on which I informed him as far as he enquired.

One of the committee in a pert manner observed, 'Then your principles are passive obedience and non-resistance.' I replied, 'No, my friend, our principles are active obedience or passive suffering.'[16]

The Leading to Reform: Levi Coffin and Lucretia Mott

Levi Coffin (1798–1877) migrated from North Carolina to Indiana, part of a movement among North Carolina Friends to leave the southern states, where slavery was legal, to territories where it was prohibited. He became a leader in the Underground Railroad, the clandestine traffic of escaped slaves on their way to Canada. His activities were controversial among some Quakers. Friends had broken the law before but publicly, during the early persecutions. Now their breach of law endangered others, not themselves, so Levi Coffin and others felt easy to act in secret so as not to endanger the safety of the refugees. Loyalty to the testimony of equality led to careful reflection on the testimony of integrity, when the traditional Quaker practice of honesty could threaten the lives and liberty of the escapees. The following excerpts from his autobiography show his trust in divine providence, his clearness about his leading to assist escaping slaves, and how his faithfulness convinced others of the rightness of the cause.

> Soon after we located at Newport, I found that we were on a line of the U.G.R.R. [Underground Railroad]. Fugitives often passed through that place, and generally stopped among the colored people. There was in that neighborhood a number of families of free colored people, mostly from North Carolina, who were the descendants of slaves who had been liberated by Friends many years before, and sent to free States at the expense of North Carolina Yearly Meeting. I learned that the fugitive slaves who took refuge with these people were often pursued and captured, the colored people not being very skillful in concealing them, or shrewd in making arrangements to forward them to Canada. I was pained to hear of the capture of these fugitives, and inquired of some of the Friends in our village why they did not take them in and secrete them, when they were pursued, and then aid them on their way to Canada? I found that they were afraid of the penalty of the law. I told them that I read in the Bible when I was a boy that it was right to take in the stranger and administer to those in distress, and that I thought it was always safe to do right. The Bible, in bidding us to feed the hungry and clothe the naked, said nothing about color, and I should try to follow out the teachings of that good book. I was willing to receive and aid as many fugitives as were disposed to come to my house. I knew that my wife's feelings and sympathies regarding this matter were the same as mine, and

that she was willing to do her part. It soon became known . . . that our house was a depot where the hunted and harassed fugitive journeying northward, on the Underground Railroad, could find succor and sympathy . . . [Others of a less courageous nature advised Levi Coffin to consider the risks to his business, his family, and his own life.] After listening quietly to these counselors, I told them that I felt no condemnation for anything that I had ever done for the fugitive slaves. If by doing my duty and endeavoring to fulfill the injunctions of the Bible, I injured my business, then let my business go. As to my safety, my life was in the hands of my Divine Master, and I felt that I had his approval. I had no fear of the danger that seemed to threaten my life or my business. If I was faithful to duty, and honest and industrious, I felt that I would be preserved, and that I could make enough to support my family . . . Many of my pro-slavery customers left me for a time, my sales were diminished, and for a while my business prospects were discouraging, yet my faith was not shaken, nor my efforts for the slaves lessened. New customers soon came in to fill the places of those who had left me . . . I was blessed in all my efforts and succeeded beyond my expectations. The Underground Railroad business increased as time advanced, and it was attended with heavy expenses, which I could not have borne had not my affairs been prosperous. I found it necessary to keep a team and a wagon always at command, to convey the fugitive slaves on their journey . . . Three principal lines from the South converged at my house . . . Seldom a week passed without our receiving passengers by this mysterious road . . . The companies varied in number, from two or three fugitives to seventeen . . . This work was kept up during the time we lived at Newport, a period of more than twenty years. The number of fugitives varied considerably in different years, but the annual average was more than one hundred.[17]

Lucretia Mott (1793–1880), born in the Quaker settlement on the island of Nantucket off the coast of Massachusetts, spent her adult years in Philadelphia, where she was active in numerous social reforms of her day, particularly the anti-slavery movement and women's rights. She spoke the following words as vocal ministry in meeting for worship, and a steno-grapher took them down. For Lucretia Mott, the Spirit of God led people to concrete action, and she called upon her hearers to imitate the deeds of Christ rather than argue about their notions of him.

> Let us keep hold of the faith that is in accordance with reason and with the intelligent dictates of the pure spirit of God. Let us ever hold up the supremacy of . . . this divine guidance, as far above all the leadings of men and the teaching of books or the veneration that is imposed by the observance of these, or by worship in meeting houses. We need to understand the worship that is more in our everyday life, that is manifested more by efforts of love and of devotion to truth and righteousness. We need to consecrate ourselves more to God and to humanity and less to forms and ceremonies and to ritual faith . . . [W]e must trust in the growing light and intelligence which is spreading over the human family and which is marking those . . . who are hungering and thirsting after greater righteousness . . . [W]oman has been so debased, so crushed, her powers of mind, her very being brought low . . . woman must avail herself of the increasing means of intelligence, education and knowledge. She must rise also in a higher sphere of spiritual existence . . . Then will the time speedily come . . . when the monopoly of the pul-pit shall no more oppress her, when marriage shall not be a means of rendering her noble nature subsidiary to man, when there shall be no assumed authority on the one part nor admitted inferiority or subjection on the other . . . I would that there were successors coming forth in this great field of reform. The Almighty is calling upon both

man and woman to open their mouths . . . to plead the
cause of the poor and needy . . . and declare the truth of
God, and this will give evidence of the divinity of their
mission just as Jesus did . . . May they then not be
afraid . . . to lift up their voices . . . to let the sound be
heard far and wide and let it go forth to the ends of the
earth; the Spirit of the Lord is come upon them and they
are called to go forth on this mission. A blessing will be to
them for they will acknowledge that the Highest has been
their mouth and wisdom . . . [that] they were a few and
feeble, but that they have been made strong and mighty in
him who is ever with his children.[18]

Poetic Prayer: Inazo Nitobe and John Greenleaf Whittier

Inazo Nitobe (1862–1933) was born to the samurai class in
Japan. He studied in the United States, where he joined
Friends, and in Germany, where he received his doctorate at
Halle. In Japan he was active in education and agricultural
reform. He served as the first Undersecretary General of the
League of Nations. He described his attraction to Quakerism
as a vehicle to reconcile Christianity with eastern thought and
mysticism: Christ as the Inner Light was incarnate in Jesus,
yet as the universal Word 'enlightened the seers of old'. The following prayer, poetic in style if not in form, weaves Christian
values from the words of Jesus in the Gospels and from the
Quaker testimonies with the ideals of Japanese neo-
Confucianism. Despite the words of this prayer, Inazo Nitobe
possessed considerable learning, held relative power, experienced fame, and had relative wealth. The 'crumbs from the
table' echoes Mark 7:28. As a Japanese person coming to
Christianity, he could identify with the Syrophoenician woman
who came to Jesus as a foreigner.

> I ask for daily bread, but not for wealth, lest I forget the
> poor.

> I ask for strength, but not for power, lest I despise the meek.
>
> I ask for wisdom, but not for learning, lest I scorn the simple.
>
> I ask for a clean name, but not for fame, lest I condemn the lowly.
>
> I ask for peace of mind, but not for idle hours, lest I fail to hearken to the call of duty.
>
> For these and much more, O Father, do I crave, knocking at thy door;
>
> and, if I dare not enter, yet Thou canst dole out the crumbs fallen from Thy table.[19]

John Greenleaf Whittier (1807–92), born to a poor Quaker farming family in Massachusetts, won considerable fame for his poetry and was probably the most widely known American Quaker of the nineteenth century. His poetic subjects ranged from the romantic admiration for nature to the moral and political issues of his day. He was a staunch abolitionist and, like Lucretia Mott, an associate of William Lloyd Garrison. The following verses are from his poem 'The Brewing of Soma', composed in 1872. The beginning of the work is sharply critical of the excessive emotionalism of the evangelical revivals. The second part of the poem, often set to music in Protestant hymnals, offers a prayer celebrating the quiet inwardness of silent worship.

> Dear Lord and Father of mankind,
> Forgive our foolish ways!
> Reclothe us in our rightful mind,
> In purer lives Thy service find,
> In deeper reverence, praise.
>
> In simple trust like theirs who heard,
> Beside the Syrian sea,
> The gracious calling of the Lord,
> Let us, like them, without a word,
> Rise up and follow Thee.

O Sabbath rest by Galilee!
O calm of hills above,
Where Jesus knelt to share with Thee
The silence of eternity,
Interpreted by love!

With that deep hush subduing all
Our words and works that drown
The tender whisper of Thy call,
As noiseless let Thy blessing fall
As fell Thy manna down.

Drop Thy still dews of quietness,
Till all our strivings cease;
Take from our souls the strain and stress,
And let our ordered lives confess
The beauty of Thy peace.

Breathe through the heats of our desire
Thy coolness and Thy balm;
Let sense be dumb, let flesh retire;
Speak through the earthquake, wind, and fire,
O still, small voice of calm![20]

'There Is a Spirit Which I Feel': James Nayler and Kenneth Boulding

The following much-loved passage from early Quaker leader James Nayler (*c.* 1617–60) is often referred to as his 'last testament'. According to early Friends, he spoke these words in the final hours of his life. After a time of ministry in London, he began to travel north, with the intention of returning home to his family in Wakefield. On the way, he was robbed and bound. Discovered in a field, he was taken to a Friend's house, where he died shortly afterwards.

There is a Spirit which I feel, that delights to do no evil, nor to revenge any wrong, but delights to endure all things in hope to enjoy its own in the end. Its hope is to outlive all wrath and contention, and to weary out all exaltation and cruelty, or whatsoever is of a nature contrary to itself. It sees to the end of all temptations. As it bears no evil in itself, so it conceives none in thoughts to any other, for its ground and spring is the mercies and forgiveness of God. Its crown is meekness, its life is everlasting love unfeigned, and takes its kingdom with entreaty, and not with contention, and keeps it by lowliness of mind. In God alone it can rejoice, though none else regard it, or can own its life. It's conceived in sorrow, and brought forth without any to pity it, nor doth it murmur at grief, and oppression. It never rejoices but through sufferings, for with the world's joy it is murthered. I found it alone, being forsaken. I have fellowship therein with them that lived in dens, and desolate places in the earth, who through death obtained this resurrection, and eternal holy life.[21]

Kenneth Boulding (1910–93), born and educated in England, spent most of his scholarly career in universities in the United States. An accomplished economist and social philosopher, he was an ardent peace researcher and an avocational poet. His series of *Nayler Sonnets* is a deeply searching response to James Nayler's final words.

'There is a spirit which I feel'

Can I, imprisoned, body-bounded, touch
The starry robe of God, and from my soul,
My tiny Part, reach forth to his great Whole,
And spread my Little to the infinite Much,
When Truth forever slips from out my clutch,
And what I take indeed, I do but dole
In cupfuls from a rimless ocean-bowl
That holds a million million million such?
And yet, some Thing that moves among the stars,
And holds the cosmos in a web of law,
Moves too in me: a hunger, a quick thaw

Of soul that liquefies the ancient bars,
As I, a member of creation, sing
The burning oneness binding everything.[22]

CONCLUSION

Each spiritual tradition has its gifts to offer the rest of humankind. Even if no single feature of that tradition is utterly unique, the various spiritual practices and attitudes can combine into a distinctive whole. Many pieces of the Quaker tradition have close relatives in other spiritual communities. Still, the question remains: what does Quaker spirituality have to offer to the contemporary world?

Our era is increasingly individualistic. Many people are aware of this, and in response they long for community. They yearn for an experience akin to what Friends have called the gathered meeting, in which we meet God when we meet one another. Friends also hold up community as the place for discernment, where we can, through attentiveness to divine guidance, assist one another in guarding against self-deception.

Quaker spirituality, at its best, avoids the pitfall of spiritual narcissism. True godliness, William Penn wrote, does not turn people 'out of the world but enables them to live better in it and excites their endeavours to mend it.'[1] The spiritual practice of the testimonies reaches out to others, hoping to renew human society and make it a place of peace, of equality, of integrity, and a materially simple life that honours our delicate ecosystem.

Today many people hunger for an integration of contemplation and social action. Spiritual seekers desire a commitment to social reform that is rooted in something deeper than a theory of social analysis. Quaker experience teaches that the quest for justice is best grounded in an inward transformation from fear and greed to love of God and neighbour.

At the risk of sounding too self-assured, Quaker spirituality addresses many yearnings of contemporary spiritual seekers: contemplative spiritual practices, honest interior watchfulness, and a commitment to non-violence. Some will feel drawn to these ideals and into community with the admittedly flawed human beings who make up the Society of Friends. For others, Quakerism may seem more like the monastic life: a calling for some but not all. The ethical ideals are demanding and, to some minds, not truly fit for the practical world.

In his *Journal*, Joseph Hoag (1762–1846) told of a conversation with a military general who challenged his pacifism. In a civil but serious debate, Joseph Hoag defended his beliefs as true to the teachings of Jesus. The general needed some time to think about the Quaker's words, when one of his soldiers came to his defence.

> The general made no answer, but sat and hung his head for some time. One of the company at length replied, 'Well, stranger, if all the world was of your mind, I would turn and follow after.' I replied, 'So then thou hast a mind to be the last man in the world to be good. I have a mind to be one of the first, and set the rest an example.' This made the general smile.[2]

Quakers would prefer that the whole world live by the testimonies, but many of us would regard it as a good start if we could make the general smile. Even though history suggests to us that we may never be large in numbers, Quakers hope to hold up worthy ideals and spiritual practices that can lead the way to those ideals. With grace, may we continue to be open to conversation with all, aspiring to practise a genuine hospitality that has characterized Christianity at its best.

NOTES

Introduction

1. Margaret Fell, 'Epistle to Friends', 1654, in Mary Garman, Judith Applegate, Margaret Benefiel, and Dortha Meredith (eds.), *Hidden in Plain Sight: Quaker Women's Writings 1650–1700* (Wallingford, Pennsylvania: Pendle Hill, 1996), p. 457.
2. Rufus M. Jones (ed.), *George Fox: An Autobiography* (Philadelphia: Ferris and Leach, 1903), vol. 1, p. 213.

1. Spiritual Ideals in Quaker History

1. Benedict of Nursia (c. 480–c. 547) was an early Christian monk. Although not among the first followers of the monastic life, who preceded him by at least two centuries, he composed a rule for monastic living that eventually became the most influential in western Christianity. Benedict was not a founder of monasticism, but he helped to shape it into an enduring institution.
2. *The Journal of George Fox*, edited by John L. Nickalls (London: Religious Society of Friends, 1975), p. 11.
3. George Fox, *Journal*, p. 19.
4. *ibid.*, pp. 27-8.
5. *ibid.*, p. 34.
6. Margaret Fell, *The Testimony of Margaret Fox Concerning Her Late Husband George Fox: Together with a Brief Account of Some of His Travels, Sufferings, and Hardships Endured for the Truth's Sake*. Printed in Mary Garman, Judith Applegate, Margaret Benefiel, and Dortha Meredith (eds.), *Hidden in Plain Sight: Quaker Women's Writings 1650–1700* (Wallingford, Pennsylvania: Pendle Hill, 1996), p. 235.
7. Margaret Fell, 'Letter to Friends, Brethren and Sisters', *1656*, in *Undaunted Zeal: The Letters of Margaret Fell*, edited by Elsa F. Glines (Richmond, Indiana: Friends United Press, 2003), p. 212.
8. George Fox, *Journal*, p. 58.
9. My comments on the Lamb's War draw heavily on Hugh Barbour,

The Quakers in Puritan England (New Haven, Connecticut: Yale University Press, 1964), pp. 102-5.

10. See, for example, John 4:14, 11:26.

11. Sarah Blackborrow, *A Visit to the Spirit in Prison* . . . (London, 1658), reprinted in Mary Garman *et al.* (eds.), *Hidden in Plain Sight*, pp. 48, 55, with some modernization of spelling and punctuation.

12. George Fox, *Journal*, p. 52.

13. *Memoirs and Letters of Richard and Elizabeth Shackleton*, edited by Mary Leadbetter (London: Charles Gilpin, 1849), p. 11.

14. *ibid.*, p. 10.

15. *ibid.*, pp. 217-18.

16. For a fuller description of John Woolman's understanding of spiritual growth, see my *A Near Sympathy: The Timeless Quaker Wisdom of John Woolman* (Richmond, Indiana: Friends United Press, 2003).

17. John Woolman, *The Journal and Major Essays of John Woolman*, edited by Phillips P. Moulton (Oxford: Oxford University Press, 1971; reprint Richmond, Indiana: Friends United Press, 1989), pp. 176-7.

18. Here it might be useful to note that 'universalism' has more than one meaning in Christian theology. Quaker universalism means that through the Inward Light, God's guiding presence is available to every human being. In other traditions, the term refers to universal salvation, that is, that everyone will in the end receive everlasting life in heaven; no one is doomed to eternal perdition. Proponents of this second kind of universalism date back at least to the third century and the writings of Origen of Alexandria. This is a distinctive theological trait of the Universalist Church in North America, which joined with the Unitarian Church in 1961, to form the Unitarian Universalist Association.

19. Sarah (Lynes) Grubb, *Letters, etc. of Sarah Grubb* (London: A.W. Bennett, 1864), p. 289.

20. Joseph John Gurney, *Essay on the Habitual Exercise of Love to God* (London: R.B. Seeley and W. Burnside, 1834), pp. 50-3.

21. For a full account of this transition, see Thomas D. Hamm, *The Transformation of American Quakerism: Orthodox Friends, 1800–1907* (Bloomington: Indiana University Press, 1988).

22. *Proceedings, Including Declaration of Christian Doctrine, of the General Conference of Friends Held In Richmond, Ind., U. S. A.* (Richmond, Indiana: Nicholson and Brothers, 1887). See page 29 for the rejection of universalism, and the dismissal of continuing revelation.

23. 'Three Friends' [Francis Frith, William E. Turner, William Pollard], *A Reasonable Faith* (London: Macmillan, 1884), pp. 6-7, 65.

2. Meeting for Worship

1. Robert Barclay, *Apology for True Christian Divinity* (Latin edition,

1676; English edition, London, 1678), Proposition 11 ('On Worship').
Section 7. (Since the *Apology* underwent numerous printings over
the centuries, it is common practice to refer to a passage by proposition and section number.)

2. Caroline E. Stephen, *Quaker Strongholds* (London: E. Hicks, jun.,
   1891), pp. 12-13.

3. Tayeko Yamanouchi, 'Ways of Worship', *Friends World News*
   (Autumn 1979), no. 113, p. 13.

4. Isaac Penington, *A Brief Account Concerning Silent Meetings, the
   Nature, Use, Intent, and Benefit of Them*. From *The Works of Isaac
   Penington, a Minister of the Gospel in the Society of Friends*
   (Sherwoods, New York: David Heston, 1863; reprint Glenside,
   Pennsylvania: Quaker Heritage Press, 1997), vol. 4, p. 47.

5. Robert Barclay, *Apology for True Christian Divinity*, Proposition 11,
   Section 7.

6. *The Quaker, Being a Series of Sermons by Members of the Society of
   Friends*, edited by Marcus Gould (Philadelphia, 1827), vol. 1, p. 47.

7. Introductions to centring prayer may be found in Thomas Keating,
   *Open Mind, Open Heart: The Contemplatives Dimension of the
   Gospel* (New York: Continuum, 1986), and Basil Pennington,
   Centering Prayer: Renewing an Ancient Christian Prayer Form (New
   York: Doubleday, 1980).

8. See William Taber, *Four Doors to Meeting for Worship* (Wallingford,
   Pennsylvania: Pendle Hill, 1992), pp. 15-16.

9. Beatrix Saxon Snell, *A Joint and Visible Worship* (Wallingford,
   Pennsylvania: Pendle Hill, 1965), p. 10.

10. George Fox, Epistle 24, in T. Canby Jones (ed.), *The Power of the Lord
    Is over All: The Pastoral Epistles of George Fox* (Richmond, Indiana:
    Friends United Press, 1989), p. 18.

11. Robert Barclay, *Apology*, Proposition 11, Section 17.

12. Caroline E. Stephen, *Light Arising: Thoughts on the Central
    Radiance* (Cambridge: W. Heffer & Sons, 1908), pp. 68-9.

13. Robert Barclay, *Apology*, Prop. 11, Section 7.

14. See *ibid*.

15. William Taber makes a distinction between a gathered meeting and
    a covered meeting which may be useful. 'In a "gathered" meeting
    most of the participants are unitedly waiting together upon God, and
    they generally feel a sense of timeless peace in this state of con-
    sciousness. In a "covered" meeting the participants also feel a special
    sense of the Divine Spirit powerfully at work among them – whether
    through spoken ministry and prayer or through the invisible, ener-
    gizing, transforming, and bonding work of the Holy Spirit.' From
    William Taber, *Four Doors to Meeting for Worship* (Wallingford,
    Pennsylvania: Pendle Hill, 1992), p. 29.

16. Thomas Kelly, 'The Gathered Meeting' (Philadelphia: Tract

Association of Friends, n.d.) reprinted in *The Eternal Promise* (Richmond, Indiana: Friends United Press, 1977), p. 72.

17. See, for example, Teruyasu Tamura, *A Zen Buddhist Encounters Quakerism* (Wallingford, Pennsylvania: Pendle Hill, 1992).

18. This is a complex matter, metaphysically speaking, since Buddhists do not believe in a permanent, enduring self. Yet the goal of the individual meditating is to achieve first of all insight for herself or himself. In Mahayana, there is the tradition of the *bodhisattva*, who vows not to enter nirvana until all sentient beings can achieve the same, yet Buddhist meditation is on the whole not a community experience, even though it may be helpful to meditate when there are others in the same meditation hall.

19. William Penn, 'Preface to the original edition of George Fox's Journal, 1694', in *The Journal of George Fox*, edited by John L. Nickalls (London: Religious Society of Friends, 1975), pp. xlii-iv.

20. Rufus M. Jones, *The Trail of Life in the Middle Years* (New York: Macmillan, 1934), p. 46.

21. L. Violet Holdsworth, *Silent Worship: The Way of Wonder* (London: Headley Brothers, 1919), pp. 77-8.

22. Samuel Bownas, *Description of the Qualifications Necessary to a Gospel Minister* (London: L. Hinde, 1750; reprint Philadelphia: Pendle Hill Publications and Tract Association of Friends, 1989), p. 99.

23. John Woolman, *The Journal and Major Essays of John Woolman*, edited by Phillips P. Moulton (New York: Oxford University Press, 1971; reprint Richmond, Indiana: Friends United Press, 1989), p. 31.

24. John Woolman, *Journal*, p. 31.

25. George Fox, *Journal*, p. 446.

26. Norman Penney (ed.), *First Publishers of Truth* (London: Headley Brothers, 1907), quoted in Hugh Barbour and Arthur O. Roberts, *Early Quaker Writings: 1650–1700* (Grand Rapids, Michigan: Eerdmans, 1973), p. 58.

27. Abram Rawlinson Barclay (ed.), *Letters of Early Friends* (London: Harvey and Darton, 1841), p. 27.

28. Cited in Barbour and Roberts, *Early Quaker Writings*, pp. 487-8; also in T. Canby Jones (ed.), *The Power of the Lord Is over All: The Pastoral Epistles of George Fox* (Richmond, Indiana: Friends United Press, 1989), pp. 9-10.

29. John Rutty, *Spiritual Diary and Soliloquies* (London: James Phillips, 1796), p. 390.

30. See the thoughtful discussion in Patricia Loring's very valuable *Listening Spirituality*, vol. 2, *Corporate Spiritual Practice Among Friends* (Washington Grove, Maryland: Openings Press 1999), pp. 127-36.

31. George Fox, 'Something Farther Concerning Silent Meetings', in *Gospel Truth Demonstrated* (London: T. Sowle, 1706), p. 103.

3. Discernment

1. This following discussion is much indebted to Hugh Barbour, *Quakers in Puritan England* (New Haven, Connecticut: Yale University Press, 1964), pp. 119-23.

2. Historians have long debated what 'nakedness' meant in that era. For what it is worth, the most current research suggests that those involved did not divest themselves of their undergarments. I am thankful to the staff at Woodbrooke Quaker Study Centre in Birmingham, England, for this information from research-in-progress.

3. See the discussion on pp. 24-5.

4. Barbour, *Quakers in Puritan England*, p. 120.

5. T. Canby Jones (ed.), *The Power of the Lord Is over All: The Pastoral Epistles of George Fox* (Richmond, Indiana: Friends United Press, 1989), *Epistle 31*, p. 306.

6. John Woolman, *The Journal and Major Essays of John Woolman*, edited by Phillips P. Moulton (New York: Oxford University Press, 1971; reprint Richmond, Indiana: Friends United Press, 1989), pp. 32-3.

7. John Woolman, *Journal*, pp. 198, 210.

8. *ibid.*, pp. 122-3.

9. *ibid.*, p. 112.

10. *ibid.*, p. 46.

11. *ibid.*, p. 52.

12. *ibid.*, p. 55.

13. *ibid.*, p. 123.

14. *ibid.*, p. 124.

15. *ibid.*, pp. 127-8.

16. *ibid.*, p. 130.

17. See *ibid.*, pp. 155-9.

18. Amelia Mott Gummere (ed.), *The Journal and Essays of John Woolman* (New York: Macmillan, 1922), p. 315.

19. See his relationships with Samuel Newby on p. 71 and John Churchman on pp. 77-8 of the Phillips Moulton edition of his *Journal*.

20. Robert Vaux, *Memoirs of the Lives of Benjamin Lay and Ralph Sandiford; Two of the Earliest Public Advocates for the Emancipation of the Enslaved Africans* (Philadelphia: Solomon W. Conrad, 1815), pp. 25-7.

21. Gummere (ed.), *The Journal and Essays of John Woolman*, p. 314.

22. John Woolman, *Journal*, edited by Phillips Moulton, p. 72.

23. Edward Burrough, 'A Testimony Concerning the Work of the Lord' (1662), printed in Abram Rawlinson Barclay (ed.), *Letters of Early Friends* (London: Harvey and Darton, 1841), p. 305.

24. I first heard this explanation from Nelson Bingham, professor of psychology at Earlham College, where he served very capably as clerk of the faculty, whose meetings are informed by Quaker practice.

25. For similar questions, see *Faith and Practice: A Book of Christian*

Discipline (Philadelphia: Philadelphia Yearly Meeting of the Religious Society of Friends, 1997), p. 27.

26. Elwood Cronk, 'Not Consensus' in *Friends Journal*, vol. 28, no. 6 (1 April 1982): 11.

27. For a description of this evolution, see Patricia Loring, *Spiritual Discernment: The Context and Goals of Clearness Committees* (Wallingford, Pennsylvania: Pendle Hill, 1992). Although I speak here from personal experience of clearness committees, Patricia Loring's work has been so influential among contemporary Friends that I gratefully acknowledge the influence of this important text.

28. Jesuit Michael J. Sheeran authored a useful study, *Beyond Majority Rule: Voteless Decisions in the Religious Society of Friends* (Philadelphia: Philadelphia Yearly Meeting of the Religious Society of Friends, 1983). Benedictine Prior Justin Duvall sojourned at the Quaker study centre Pendle Hill to learn about Quaker methods of decision-making. Suzanne G. Farnham's *Listening Hearts: Discerning Call in Community* (Ridgefield, Connecticut: Morehouse, 1996) discusses Quaker models for discernment, drawing on Michael Sheeran's work. Associates of Shalem Institute for Spiritual Formation, an ecumenical Christian organization for contemplative spirituality, have told me that Quaker understandings have influenced Shalem's teaching on discernment, largely through the influence of Douglas Steere, with whom the founders of Shalem consulted as they were establishing the programme. Monteze Snyder, a Quaker and professor of management, led a team that included Cheryl Gibbs, Susan A. Hillmann, Trayce N. Peterson, Joanna Schofield and George H. Watson, to produce their volume *Building Consensus: Conflict and Unity* (Richmond, Indiana: Earlham Press, 2001), which explains Quaker decision-making for the management community.

4. Nurturing the Inward Life

1. *Faith and Practice of New England Yearly Meeting of Friends: Book of Discipline* (Worcester, Massachusetts: New England Yearly Meeting of Friends, 1986), p. 21.

2. The chief source was the *Short and Simple Method of Prayer (Le moyen court et très facile de faire oraison)* by Jeanne Marie Bouvier de la Motte Guyon, usually referred to simply as Madame Guyon. The editors also drew on the *Maxims of the Saints on the Inner Life (Explication des maximes des saints sur la vie intérieure)* of François de Saligne de La Mothe Fénelon and *Spiritual Guide (Guía espiritual)* of Miguel de Molinos.

3. Sarah (Lynes) Grubb, *Letters, etc. of Sarah Grubb* (London: A.W. Bennett, 1864), p. 152. See also Rufus M. Jones, *The Later Periods of Quakerism* (London: Macmillan 1921), vol. 1, p. 58.

4. *A Guide to True Peace: Or, a Method of Attaining to Inward and*

Spiritual Prayer, Compiled Chiefly from the Writings of Fenelon, Archbishop of Cambray, Lady Guion, and Michael de Molinos (Wallingford, Pennsylvania: Pendle Hill, 1979). This edition is the latest of many.

5. *ibid.*, p. xiv. To what extent they have 'Quakerised' the original texts remains a question for further study.

6. *ibid.*, p. 14.

7. *ibid.*, p. 14.

8. *ibid.*, p. 24.

9. *ibid.*, pp. 24-5.

10. *ibid.*, p. 33.

11. *ibid.*, p. 97.

12. *ibid.*, p. 27.

13. *ibid.*, p. 39.

14. *ibid.*, p. 46.

15. *ibid.*, pp. 66, 74, 64, 64, 84, and 87, respectively.

16. Thomas Keating makes such a distinction, referring to one as 'the sacred word' and the other as 'active prayer', in *Open Mind, Open Heart, The Contemplative Dimension of the Gospel* (New York: Continuum, 1986), pp. 133-5.

17. Thomas R. Kelly, *A Testament of Devotion* (New York: Harper and Row, 1941), p. 35.

18. *ibid.*, pp. 31-2.

19. *ibid.*, pp. 38-9.

20. *ibid.*, p. 61.

21. *ibid.*, p. 39.

22. *ibid.*, pp. 38-1.

23. This is not to deny the impact of Rufus Jones, whose influence during his lifetime was greater than that of his student Thomas Kelly. Yet Rufus Jones wrote over fifty books, no single one of which has been as popular as *A Testament of Devotion*, though their cumulative effect has been greater.

24. Quaker letters of spiritual counsel invite a comparison with those from other traditions, such as their near contemporaries in France, Jane de Chantal and Francis de Sales.

25. George Fox, Epistle 10, printed in Hugh Barbour and Arthur O. Roberts, *Early Quaker Writings: 1650–1700* (Grand Rapids, Michigan: Eerdmans, 1973), p. 487, also printed in T. Canby Jones, (ed.), *The Power of the Lord Is Over All: The Pastoral Letters of George Fox* (Richmond, Indiana: Friends United Press, 1989), p. 7.

26. *The Journal of George Fox*, edited by John L. Nickalls (London: Religious Society of Friends, 1975), pp. 346-8.

27. James Nayler, 'Letter from Appleby Prison, February 1653', from Geoffrey F. Nuttall, 'The Letters of James Nayler', in *The Lamb's War: Quaker Essays to Honor Hugh Barbour*, edited by Michael L.

Birkel and John W. Newman (Richmond, Indiana: Earlham College Press, 1992), pp. 46-7.

28. Richard Shackleton, 'Letter to John Conran, 1772', in *Memoirs and Letters of Richard and Elizabeth Shackleton*, edited by Mary Leadbetter (London: Charles Gilpin, 1849), pp. 77-9.

29. George Fox, Epistle 227, in T. Canby Jones (ed.), *The Power of the Lord Is Over All: The Pastoral Letters of George Fox* (Richmond, Indiana: Friends United Press, 1989), pp. 185-6.

30. For a study of the genre of the journal among Friends, see Howard H. Brinton, *Quaker Journals: Varieties of Religious Experience Among Friends* (Wallingford, Pennsylvania: Pendle Hill, 1972).

31. Elizabeth Stirredge, *Strength in Weakness Manifest in the Life, Various Trials, and Christian Testimony, of That Faithful Servant and Handmaid of the Lord, Elizabeth Stirredge* (London: J. Sowle, 1711).

32. *Short Relation of Some of the Cruel Sufferings for the Truth's Sake of Katharine Evans and Sarah Cheevers, in the Inquisition in the Isle of Malta* (London, 1662), reprinted in Mary Garman *et al.* (eds.), *Hidden in Plain Sight: Quaker Women's Writings 1650–1700* (Wallingford, Pennsylvania: Pendle Hill, 1996), pp. 172-209.

33. Cyrus G. Pringle, *The Civil War Diary of Cyrus Pringle*, with a foreword by Henry J. Cadbury (Wallingford, Pennsylvania: Pendle Hill, 1962), remains in print. An earlier edition is *The Record of a Quaker Conscience: Cyrus Pringle's Diary*, with an introduction by Rufus M. Jones (New York: Macmillan, 1918).

34. Elizabeth Ashbridge, *Some account of the early part of the life of Elizabeth Ashbridge . . . Written by Herself* (Philadelphia: Benjamin and Thomas Kite, 1807), p. 15.

35. Mary Penington, *Some Account of Circumstances in the Life of Mary Penington* (London: Harvey and Darton, 1821); reprinted in Mary Garman *et al.* (eds.), *Hidden in Plain Sight*, p. 219.

36. David Ferris, *Memoirs of the Life of David Ferris* (Philadelphia: John Simons, 1825), pp. 74-5; recently reprinted as *Resistance and Obedience to God: Memoirs of David Ferris (1707–1779)*, edited by Martha Paxson Grundy (Philadelphia: Friends General Conference, 2001).

37. *The Journals of the Lives and Travels of Samuel Bownas and John Richardson* (London: William Dunlap, 1759), p. 115.

38. John Woolman, *The Journal and Major Essays of John Woolman*, ed. Phillips P. Moulton (Oxford: Oxford University Press, 1971; reprint Richmond, Indiana: Friends United Press, 1989), pp. 185-6.

39. For a fuller discussion of this passage, see my 'John Woolman on the Cross', in *The Lamb's War: Quaker Essays to Honor Hugh Barbour*, edited by Michael L. Birkel and John W. Newman (Richmond, Indiana: Earlham College Press, 1992), pp. 93-100.

40. By the eighteenth century, Friends who were recognized as having

gifts in ministry were publicly 'recorded' or 'acknowledged' by their local meetings.

41. Robert Barclay, *Apology for True Christian Divinity* (London, 1678), Proposition 10, 'On the Ministry', Section 26.

42. This is a generalization. Ministers continued to 'appoint meetings' with non-Quakers, but this was not often at the centre of their work, to judge from the journals of ministers' travels.

43. John Woolman, *Journal*, p. 131.

44. See David Knowles, *Christian Monasticism* (New York: McGraw-Hill, 1969), p. 32.

45. At the time of their travelling together, Catherine Phillips was the younger of the two, but because Mary Peisley died shortly thereafter and Catherine Phillips lived much longer and wrote her journal years later, her journal is the more reflective of the two works.

46. Catherine Phillips, *Memoirs of the Life of Catherine Phillips* (London: J. Phillips and son, 1797), p. 154.

47. *ibid.*, p. 136.

48. *ibid.*, p. 137.

49. *ibid.*, p. 50.

50. *ibid.*, pp. 118-19.

51. *ibid.*, p. 130.

52. Mary Peisley Neale, *Some Account of the Life and Religious Exercises of Mary Neale, formerly Peisley* (Philadelphia: Friends Book Store, 1860), pp. 163-4. Here I would like to acknowledge my gratitude to my colleague and friend Mary Garman for enlightening conversation on the friendship of these two ministers.

53. *Short Relation of Some of the Cruel Sufferings for the Truth's Sake of Katharine Evans and Sarah Cheevers, in the Inquisition in the Isle of Malta* (London, 1662); reprinted in Mary Garman *et al.* (eds.), *Hidden in Plain Sight*, pp. 172-209.

54. *Memoirs of the Life and Gospel Labors of Stephen Grellet* (Philadelphia: Henry Longstreth, 1864), vol. 2, p. 79.

55. Meetings with pastors continued to record ministers, but since they served a central role in leading their congregations, they tended not to travel. Conservative Friends in the Wilburite tradition, whose worship is not programmed or led by pastors, have continued to acknowledge ministers in the old style. Conservative Friends have preserved many Quaker traditions, such as collective written responses to the queries (see below), and have kept alive the practice of elders. Although small in numbers, Conservative Friends have been a leaven in wider Quakerism and have contributed in important ways to the present renewal of Quaker spirituality.

56. Robert Barclay, *Apology*, Proposition 10, Section 26.

57. John Rutty, *Spiritual Diary and Soliloquies* (London: James Phillips, 1796), p. 81.

58. Philadelphia Yearly Meeting minutes of 1723, quoted in Howard H.

Brinton, *Friends for 300 Years* (New York: Harper and Brothers, 1952), p. 93.

59. Postscript to an Epistle to 'the brethren in the north' issued by a meeting of elders at Balby, 1656, cited in *Quaker Faith & Practice: The Book of Christian Discipline of the Yearly Meeting of the Religious Society of Friends (Quakers) in Britain* (London: The Yearly Meeting of the Religious Society of Friends [Quakers] in Britain, 1995), 1.01. This advice from the elders at Balby is found in the books of faith and practice of many yearly meetings.

60. From Philadelphia Yearly Meeting, *Christian and Brotherly Advices, 1743*, cited in Hugh Barbour and J. William Frost, *The Quakers* (Richmond, Indiana: Friends United Press, 1994), p. 109.

61. *Quaker Faith & Practice: The Book of Christian Discipline of the Yearly Meeting of the Religious Society of Friends (Quakers) in Britain* (London: The Yearly Meeting of the Religious Society of Friends [Quakers] in Britain, 1995), 1.02.

5. The Testimonies

1. William Penn, *A Treatise of Oaths, Containing Several Weighty Reasons Why the People Call'd Quakers Refuse to Swear* (n.p., 1675), p. 24.

2. *The Journal of George Fox*, edited by John L. Nickalls (London: Religious Society of Friends, 1975), p. 7.

3. *ibid.*, p. 9.

4. 'And as man and woman are restored again, by Christ, up into the image of God, they both have dominion again in righteousness and holiness and are helps' meet, as before the fall.' Epistle 313, in T. Canby Jones (ed.), *The Power of the Lord Is over All: The Pastoral Epistles of George Fox* (Richmond, Indiana: Friends United Press, 1989), p. 311.

5. Epistle 291, *The Power of the Lord*, p. 286.

6. Epistle 320, *The Power of the Lord*, p. 32 – see also Epistle 360, pp. 376-9.

7. Margaret Fell, *Women's Speaking Justified, Proved, and Allowed of by the Scriptures, All such as speak by the Spirit and Power of the Lord Jesus. And how Women were the first that Preached the Tidings of the Resurrection of Jesus, and were sent by Christ's own Command, before he Ascended to the Father* (London, 1666; reprint: Amherst, Massachusetts: Mosher Book & Tract Committee, New England Yearly Meeting of Friends, 1980), p. 3.

8. *ibid.*, p. 11.

9. Elizabeth Bathurst, *The Sayings of Women* (London, 1663); reprinted in Mary Garman, Judith Applegate, Margaret Benefiel, and Dortha Meredith (eds.), *Hidden in Plain Sight: Quaker Women's Writings 1650–1700* (Wallingford, Pennsylvania: Pendle Hill, 1996), p. 435.

10. *ibid.*, p. 440.
11. George Fox, *Journal*, p. 37.
12. Robert Barclay, *Apology for True Christian Divinity* (Latin edition, 1676, English edition London, 1678), Proposition 15, Section 3.
13. *ibid.*, Proposition 15, Introductory Thesis.
14. George Fox, *Journal*, p. 26.
15. *ibid.*, p. 49.
16. *ibid.*, p. 66.
17. John Woolman, *The Journal and Major Essays of John Woolman*, edited by Phillips P. Moulton (New York: Oxford University Press, 1971; reprint Richmond, Indiana: Friends United Press, 1989), p.127.
18. See Helen Bayes, *Respecting the Rights of Children and Young People: A New Perspective on Quaker Faith and Practice*, The 2003 James Backhouse Lecture (Armandale North, Victoria: Religious Society of Friends [Quakers] in Australia, 2003).
19. William Penn, *Some Fruits of Solitude* (London, 1693), Maxim 67; reprinted in Hugh S. Barbour, *William Penn on Religion and Ethics: The Emergence of Liberal Quakerism* (Lewiston, New York: The Edwin Mellen Press, 1991), vol. 2., p. 524.
20. Margaret Fell, 'Epistle against Uniform Quaker Costume', 1700, in Hugh Barbour, (ed.), *Margaret Fell Speaking* (Wallingford, Pennsylvania: Pendle Hill, 1976), p. 32.
21. See Frederick B. Tolles' classic study, *Meeting House and Counting House* (Chapel Hill, North Carolina: University of North Carolina Press, 1948).
22. John Woolman, *Journal*, p. 35.
23. John Woolman, 'Plea for the Poor', in *The Journal and Major Essays*, p. 255.
24. *ibid.*, p. 241.
25. George Fox, *Journal*, p. 51.
26. *ibid.*, p. 65.
27. See the Epistle of James 3:17–4:2.
28. William Dewsbury, *Works*, 1689. Cited in *Quaker Faith & Practice: The Book of Christian Discipline of the Yearly Meeting of the Religious Society of Friends (Quakers) in Britain* (London: The Yearly Meeting of the Religious Society of Friends [Quakers] in Britain, 1995), 19.45.
29. James Nayler, *The Lamb's War against the Man of Sin*, excerpted in *Early Quaker Writings*, edited by Hugh Barbour and Arthur Roberts (Grand Rapids, Michigan: Eerdmans, 1974), pp. 104-16.
30. Margaret Fell, 'A Declaration and an Information from us, the People of God Called Quakers, to the . . . King and Both Houses of Parliament', 1660, in *A brief collection of remarkable passages...relating to...that ancient, eminent, and faithful servant of the Lord, Margaret Fell* . . . (London: J. Sowle, 1710), pp. 208-9.
31. Elise Boulding, *One Small Plot of Heaven: Reflections on Family Life*

by a Quaker Sociologist (Wallingford, Pennsylvania: Pendle Hill, 1989), pp. 159, 199, respectively.

32. Rufus M. Jones, *Finding the Trail of Life* (New York: Macmillan, 1926), pp. 21-2.

6. The Facing Bench

1. For a discussion of her use of biblical language in this passage, see my 'Reading Scripture with Dorothy White', *Quaker Religious Thought* 97, vol. 30, no. 3 (September 2001), 55-62.

2. Dorothy White, *A Trumpet Sounded out of the Holy City, Proclaiming Deliverance to the Captives, Sounding Forth the Redemption of Sion, which hasteneth . . .* (1662). From *Hidden in Plain Sight: Quaker Women's Writings 1650–1700*, edited by Mary Garman *et al.* (eds.) (Wallingford, Pennsylvania: Pendle Hill, 1996), pp. 147-8, with some modernization of orthography.

3. Rufus M. Jones, *The Inner Life* (New York: Macmillan, 1916), pp. 97-101.

4. Isaac Penington, *A Brief Account Concerning Silent Meetings, the Nature, Use, Intent, and Benefit of Them.* From *The Works of Isaac Penington, a Minister of the Gospel in the Society of Friends* (Sherwoods, New York: David Heston, 1863; reprint Glenside, Pennsylvania: Quaker Heritage Press, 1997), vol. 4, p. 48.

5. Howard H. Brinton, *Friends for 300 Years* (New York: Harper and Bros., 1952; reprint Wallingford, Pennsylvania : Pendle Hill 1965), pp. 74–5.

6. 'Friends and World Religions' in *Sharing Our Quaker Faith*, edited by Edwin B. Bronner (Birmingham, England and Philadelphia, Pennsylvania: Friends World Committee for Consultation, 1959), pp. 94-108.

7. Ham Sok Hon, *Talrachinunm Sekyeui Hankil Wieso* [On the Open Road in a Changing World] (Seoul: Hankilsa, 1988), p. 328, cited in Kim Sung Soo, 'Ham Sok Hon's Understanding of Taoism and Quakerism', in *An Anthology of Ham Sok Hon*, edited by The Ham Sok Hon Memorial Foundation (Seoul: Samin Books, 2001), p. 304.

8. Ham Sok Hon, *Hanguk Kitokkyonun Muotul Haryonunka* [What Is Christianity Going to Do in Korea], (Seoul: Hankilsa, 1989), p. 171, cited in Kim Sung Soo, 'Ham Sok Hon's Understanding of Taoism and Quakerism', in *An Anthology of Ham Sok Hon*, edited by The Ham Sok Hon Memorial Foundation, p. 308.

9. Ham Sok Hon, *Kicked by God*, translated by David E. Ross, originally published by the Wider Quaker Fellowship of the Friends World Committee, Philadelphia, 1969, reprinted in *An Anthology of Ham Sok Hon*, edited by The Ham Sok Hon Memorial Foundation, pp. 120-1.

10. Han Young Sang, 'War Is the Most Extreme Luxury' [Interview with Ham Sok Hon], translated by Kwahk Young Do and assisted by Lloyd

Bailey, originally published in *Madang* (May 1983), reprinted in *An Anthology of Ham Sok Hon*, edited by The Ham Sok Hon Memorial Foundation, p. 55.

11. Ham Sok Hon, *Sop'ungui Norae* [The Ode of the West Wind] (Seoul: Hankilsa, 1989), p. 216, cited in Kim Sung Soo, 'Ham Sok Hon's Understanding of Taoism and Quakerism', in *An Anthology of Ham Sok Hon*, edited by The Ham Sok Hon Memorial Foundation, p. 309.

12. Ham Sok Hon, *Turyowo Malgo Oech'ila* [Speak Out Fearlessly] (Seoul: Hankilsa, 1988), p. 380, cited in Kim Sung Soo, 'Ham Sok Hon's Understanding of Taoism and Quakerism', in *An Anthology of Ham Sok Hon*, edited by The Ham Sok Hon Memorial Foundation, p. 309, bracketed words in the original.

13. Samuel Bownas, *A Description of the Qualifications Necessary to a Gospel Minister* (London: Printed at the Bible in George-Yard, 1767; reprint Philadelphia: Pendle Hill Publications and the Tract Association of Friends, 1989), p. 7.

14. Sandra Cronk, *Dark Night Journey: Inward Re-patterning Toward a Life Centered in God* (Wallingford, Pennsylvania: Pendle Hill, 1991), pp. 47-9.

15. *The Journal of George Fox*, edited by John L. Nickalls (London: Religious Society of Friends, 1975), pp. 399-400, bracketed words in the original.

16. William Rotch, *Memorandum Written in the Eightieth Year of His Age* (Boston: Houghton Mifflin, 1916), pp. 3-5, with some modernization of orthography.

17. Levi Coffin, *Reminiscences of Levi Coffin* (Cincinnati, Ohio: Robert Clark, 1880), pp. 107-13.

18. Lucretia Mott, 'Abuses and Uses of the Bible', a Sermon delivered at Cherry Street Meeting, Philadelphia, Eleventh Month, Fourth, 1849. Edited from Swarthmore Friends Collection MSS 047, Swarthmore College, Swarthmore, Pennsylvania. Also available in *Lucretia Mott: Her Complete Speeches and Sermons*, edited by Dana Greene (New York and Toronto: Edwin Mellen, 1980).

19. Inazo Nitobe, 'A Supplication', from *Thoughts and Essays* (1909), reprinted in *Selections from Inazo Nitobe's Writings [Nitobe Hakushi bunshu]*, edited by Tadao Yanaihara ([Tokyo]: The Nitobe Memorial Fund, 1936), p. 159.

20. John Greenleaf Whittier, *The Complete Poetical Works of John Greenleaf Whittier*, edited by Horace E. Scudder (Boston and New York: Houghton and Mifflin; Cambridge: Riverside Press, 1894), p. 450.

21. Epistle 89, 'To Friends', edited by Geoffrey F. Nuttall in 'The Letters of James Nayler', in *The Lamb's War: Quaker Essays to Honor Hugh Barbour*, edited by Michael L. Birkel and John W. Newman (Richmond, Indiana: Earlham College Press, 1992), pp. 74-5, with some modernization of orthography.

22. Kenneth E. Boulding, *There Is a Spirit: The Nayler Sonnets* (New York: Fellowship Publications, [1945]; reprinted Wallingford, Pennsylvania: Pendle Hill, 1998), p. 8.

Conclusion

1. William Penn, *No Cross, No Crown*, second edition (London: Benjamin Clark, 1682; reprint York: William Sessions, 1981), chapter 5, section 12, p. 63.
2. Joseph Hoag, *Journal of the Life of Joseph Hoag, an Eminent Minister of the Gospel, in the Society of Friends* (Auburn, New York: Knapp and Peck, 1861), p. 201.

WORKS CITED

Ashbridge, Elizabeth, *Some account of the early part of the life of Elizabeth Ashbridge . . . Written by Herself* (Philadelphia: Benjamin and Thomas Kite, 1807)

[Backhouse, William, and James Janson], *A Guide to True Peace: Or, a Method of Attaining to Inward and Spiritual Prayer, Compiled Chiefly from the Writings of Fenelon, Archbishop of Cambray, Lady Guion, and Michael de Molinos* (Wallingford, Pennsylvania: Pendle Hill, 1979)

Barbour, Hugh S., *The Quakers in Puritan England* (New Haven, Connecticut: Yale University Press, 1964)

 William Penn on Religion and Ethics: The Emergence of Liberal Quakerism (Lewiston, New York: The Edwin Mellen Press, 1991)

 (ed.), *Margaret Fell Speaking* (Wallingford, Pennsylvania: Pendle Hill, 1976)

Barbour, Hugh, and Arthur O. Roberts, *Early Quaker Writings*: 1650–1700 (Grand Rapids, Michigan: Eerdmans, 1973)

Barbour, Hugh, and J. William Frost, *The Quakers* (Richmond, Indiana: Friends United Press, 1994)

Barclay, Abram Rawlinson (ed.), *Letters of Early Friends* (London: Harvey and Darton, 1841)

Barclay, Robert, *Apology for True Christian Divinity* (Latin edition, 1676; English edition, London, 1678)

Bayes, Helen, *Respecting the Rights of Children and Young People: A New Perspective on Quaker Faith and Practice*, The 2003 James Backhouse Lecture (Armandale North, Victoria: Religious Society of Friends [Quakers] in Australia, 2003)

Birkel, Michael L., *A Near Sympathy: The Timeless Quaker Wisdom of John Woolman* (Richmond, Indiana: Friends United Press, 2003)

 'Reading Scripture with Dorothy White', *Quaker Religious Thought* 97, vol. 30, no. 3 (September 2001): 55-62

Boulding, Elise, *One Small Plot of Heaven: Reflections on Family Life by a Quaker Sociologist* (Wallingford, Pennsylvania: Pendle Hill, 1989)

Boulding, Kenneth E., *There Is a Spirit: The Nayler Sonnets* (New York: Fellowship Publications, [1945]; reprint Wallingford, Pennsylvania: Pendle Hill, 1998)

Bownas, Samuel, *Description of the Qualifications Necessary to a Gospel Minister* (London: L. Hinde, 1750; reprint Philadelphia: Pendle Hill Publications and Tract Association of Friends, 1989)

Bownas, Samuel, and John Richardson, *The Journals of the Lives and Travels of Samuel Bownas and John Richardson* (London: William Dunlap, 1759)

Brinton, Howard H., *Friends for 300 Years* (New York: Harper and Brothers, 1952)

Quaker Journals: Varieties of Religious Experience Among Friends (Wallingford, Pennsylvania: Pendle Hill, 1972)

Bronner, Edwin B. (ed.), *Sharing Our Quaker Faith* (Birmingham, England and Philadelphia, Pennsylvania: Friends World Committee for Consultation, 1959)

Coffin, Levi, *Reminiscences of Levi Coffin* (Cincinnati, Ohio: Robert Clark, 1880)

Cronk, Elwood, 'Not Consensus' in *Friends Journal*, vol. 28, no. 6 (1 April 1982): 11-13

Cronk, Sandra, *Dark Night Journey: Inward Re-patterning Toward a Life Centered in God* (Wallingford, Pennsylvania: Pendle Hill, 1991)

Fell, Margaret, 'A Declaration and an Information from us, the People of God Called Quakers, to the ... King and Both Houses of Parliament', 1660, in *A brief collection of remarkable passages . . . of that ancient, eminent, and faithful servant of the Lord, Margaret Fell . . .* (London: J. Sowle, 1710)

Women's Speaking Justified, Proved, and Allowed of by the Scriptures, . . . (London, 1666; reprint Amherst, Mass.: Mosher Book & Tract Committee, New England Yearly Meeting of Friends, 1980)

Ferris, David, *Memoirs of the Life of David Ferris* (Philadelphia: John Simons, 1825); reprinted as *Resistance and Obedience to God: Memoirs of David Ferris (1707–1779)*, edited by Martha Paxson Grundy (Philadelphia: Friends General Conference, 2001)

Fox, George, *Gospel Truth Demonstrated* (London: T. Sowle, 1706)

Garman, Mary, Judith Applegate, Margaret Benefiel, and Dortha Meredith (eds.), *Hidden in Plain Sight: Quaker Women's Writings 1650–1700* (Wallingford, Pennsylvania: Pendle Hill, 1996)

Glines, Elsa F. (ed.), *Undaunted Zeal: The Letters of Margaret Fell* (Richmond, Indiana: Friends United Press, 2003)

Gould, Marcus (ed.), *The Quaker, Being a Series of Sermons by Members of the Society of Friends* (Philadelphia, 1827)

Grellet, Stephen, *Memoirs of the Life and Gospel Labors of Stephen Grellet* (Philadelphia: Henry Longstreth, 1864)

Grubb, Sarah (Lynes), *Letters, etc. of Sarah Grubb* (London: A.W. Bennett, 1864)

Gummere, Amelia Mott (ed.), *The Journal and Essays of John Woolman* (New York: Macmillan, 1922)

Gurney, Joseph John, *Essay on the Habitual Exercise of Love to God* (London: R.B. Seeley and W. Burnside, 1834)

Ham Sok Hon Memorial Foundation (ed.), *An Anthology of Ham Sok Hon* (Seoul: Samin Books, 2001)

Hamm, Thomas D., *The Transformation of American Quakerism; Orthodox Friends, 1800–1907* (Bloomington: Indiana University Press, 1988)

Hoag, Joseph, *Journal of the Life of Joseph Hoag, an Eminent Minister of the Gospel, in the Society of Friends* (Auburn, New York: Knapp and Peck, 1861)

Holdsworth, L. Violet, *Silent Worship: The Way of Wonder* (London: Headley Brothers, 1919)

Jones, Rufus M., *The Inner Life* (New York: Macmillan, 1916)
  Later Periods of Quakerism (London: Macmillan, 1921)
  Finding the Trail of Life (New York: Macmillan, 1926)
  The Trail of Life in the Middle Years (New York: Macmillan, 1934)
  (ed.), *George Fox: An Autobiography* (Philadelphia: Ferris and Leach, 1903)

Jones, T. Canby (ed.), *The Power of the Lord Is over All: The Pastoral Epistles of George Fox* (Richmond, Indiana: Friends United Press, 1989)

Keating, Thomas, *Open Mind, Open Heart: The Contemplatives Dimension of the Gospel* (New York: Continuum, 1986)

Kelly, Thomas, 'The Gathered Meeting' (Philadelphia: Tract Association of Friends, n.d.); reprinted in *The Eternal Promise* (Richmond, Indiana: Friends United Press, 1977)

Knowles, David, *Christian Monasticism* (New York: McGraw-Hill, 1969)

Leadbetter, Mary (ed.), *Memoirs and Letters of Richard and Elizabeth Shackleton* (London: Charles Gilpin, 1849)

Loring, Patricia, *Spiritual Discernment: The Context and Goals of Clearness Committees* (Wallingford, Pennsylvania: Pendle Hill, 1992)
  Listening Spirituality (Washington Grove, Maryland: Openings Press, 1999)

Mott, Lucretia, 'Abuses and Uses of the Bible', a Sermon delivered at Cherry Street Meeting, Philadelphia, Eleventh Month, Fourth, 1849. Edited from Swarthmore Friends Collection MSS 047, Swarthmore College, Swarthmore, Pennsylvania

Neale, Mary Peisley, *Some Account of the Life and Religious Exercises of Mary Neale, formerly Peisley* (Philadelphia: Friends Book Store, 1860)

New England Yearly Meeting of Friends, *Faith and Practice of New England Yearly Meeting of Friends: Book of Discipline* (Worcester, Massachusetts: New England Yearly Meeting of Friends, 1986)

Nickalls, John L. (ed.), *The Journal of George Fox* (London: Religious Society of Friends, 1975)

Nitobe, Inazo, *Selections from Inazo Nitobe's Writings [Nitobe Hakushi bunshu]*, edited by Tadao Yanaihara ([Tokyo]: The Nitobe Memorial Fund, 1936)

Nuttall, Geoffrey F., 'The Letters of James Nayler', in *The Lamb's War: Quaker Essays to Honor Hugh Barbour*, edited by Michael L. Birkel and John W. Newman (Richmond, Indiana: Earlham College Press, 1992): 38-75

Penington, Isaac, *The Works of Isaac Penington, a Minister of the Gospel in the Society of Friends* (Sherwoods, New York: David Heston, 1863; reprint Glenside, Pennsylvania: Quaker Heritage Press, 1997)

Penn, William, *A Treatise of Oaths, Containing Several Weighty Reasons Why the People Call'd Quakers Refuse to Swear* (n.p., 1675)
   No Cross, No Crown, second edition (London: Benjamin Clark, 1682; reprint York: William Sessions, 1981)

Penney, Norman (ed.), *First Publishers of Truth* (London: Headley Brothers, 1907)

Philadelphia Yearly Meeting of the Religious Society of Friends, *Faith and Practice: A Book of Christian Discipline* (Philadelphia: Philadelphia Yearly Meeting of the Religious Society of Friends, 1997)

Moulton, Phillips P. (ed.), *The Journal and Major Essays of John Woolman* (Oxford: Oxford University Press, 1971; reprint Richmond, Indiana: Friends United Press, 1989)

Phillips, Catherine Payton, *Memoirs of the Life of Catherine Phillips* (London: J. Phillips and son, 1797)

Pringle, Cyrus G., *The Civil War Diary of Cyrus Pringle*, with a foreword by Henry J. Cadbury (Wallingford, Pennsylvania: Pendle Hill, 1962)

Proceedings, Including Declaration of Christian Doctrine, of the General Conference of Friends Held In Richmond, Ind., U.S.A. (Richmond, Indiana: Nicholson and Brothers, 1887)

The Quaker, Being a Series of Sermons by Members of the Society of Friends, edited by Marcus Gould (Philadelphia, 1827)

Rotch, William, *Memorandum Written in the Eightieth Year of His Age* (Boston: Houghton and Mifflin, 1916)

Rutty, John, *Spiritual Diary and Soliloquies* (London: James Phillips, 1796)

Scudder, Horace E. (ed.), *The Complete Poetical Works of John Greenleaf Whittier* (Boston and New York: Houghton and Mifflin; Cambridge: Riverside Press, 1894)

Snell, Beatrix Saxon, *A Joint and Visible Worship* (Wallingford, Pennsylvania: Pendle Hill, 1965)

Stephen, Caroline E., *Quaker Strongholds* (London: E. Hicks, jun., 1891)
   Light Arising: Thoughts on the Central Radiance (Cambridge: W. Heffer & Sons, 1908)

Stirredge, Elizabeth, *Strength in Weakness Manifest in the Life, Various Trials, and Christian Testimony, of That Faithful Servant and Handmaid of the Lord, Elizabeth Stirredge* (London: J. Sowle, 1711)

Taber, William, *Four Doors to Meeting for Worship* (Wallingford, Pennsylvania: Pendle Hill, 1992)

Tamura, Teruyasu, *A Zen Buddhist Encounters Quakerism* (Wallingford, Pennsylvania: Pendle Hill, 1992)

The Yearly Meeting of the Religious Society of Friends [Quakers] in Britain, *Quaker Faith & Practice: The Book of Christian Discipline of the Yearly Meeting of the Religious Society of Friends (Quakers) in Britain* (London: The Yearly Meeting of the Religious Society of Friends [Quakers] in Britain, 1995)

'Three Friends' [Francis Frith, William E. Turner, William Pollard], *A Reasonable Faith* (London: Macmillan, 1884)

Tolles, Frederick B., *Meeting House and Counting House* (Chapel Hill, North Carolina: University of North Carolina Press, 1948)

Vaux, Robert, *Memoirs of the Lives of Benjamin Lay and Ralph Sandiford; Two of the Earliest Public Advocates for the Emancipation of the Enslaved Africans* (Philadelphia: Solomon W. Conrad, 1815)

Yamanouchi, Tayeko, 'Ways of Worship', *Friends World News* (Autumn 1979), no. 113: 13-14

Many of the works of earlier Friends are now available on-line. The Digital Quaker Collection at the Earlham School of Religion is a valuable source (http://esr.earlham.edu/dqc/). Additional digital resources, including numerous writings of historical Friends, can be found at www.quaker.org.